Pots, Tubs & Containers

Pots, Tubs & Containers

GRAHAM STRONG

MEREHURST

*To my sons Lewis and Sam, for restricting the
devastation to the top part of the garden; and
to Sally, for humouring me despite those
missed summer holidays*

First published 1997 by Merehurst Limited,
Ferry House, 51–57 Lacy Road, Putney, London SW15 1PR

Text copyright © Merehurst Limited 1997
Photography copyright © Graham Strong 1997

ISBN 1-85391 635 8

A catalogue record of this book is available from the British Library.

Typeset and edited by Joanna Chisholm
Designed by Maggie Aldred
Photography by Graham Strong
Colour separation by Bright Arts (HK) Limited
Printed by Olivotto, Italy

CONTENTS

INTRODUCTION

Growing plants in containers has to be one of the most enjoyable, relaxing and creative forms of gardening you could ever wish for. The more effort you put into this hobby, the more satisfaction you get.

My pleasure comes from such a wide range of container plants – as you'll see throughout this book – that it's hard to pick out favourites. You may however detect an underlying desire to encourage gardeners to be a little more adventurous in their plant selections. After all, almost anything will grow in a container, so don't be tied down to just run-of-the-mill summer bedding plants and don't miss out on the excitement you can generate in spring, autumn and winter, too.

Try to think of your container display as the most mobile part of your garden decor: one that can be moved about, restaged and added to throughout the seasons. As a garden designer, as well as a keen gardener, I have seen many times how a few well-placed pots can transform any type of plot. They breathe life into bare patios or stark walls and balconies and give a welcome focal point, especially around doors, windows and seats.

Nowadays, you'll find an almost bewildering array of plants and containers on sale. Don't worry. I've picked out some winning partnerships to help you: plants that have many qualities such as ease of growth, long flowering period and ravishing colours and which can be grown in anything from a sophisticated urn or terracotta pot to a disposable receptacle.

Sometimes you can buy all you need for an instant potful of colour from a single visit to your local garden retailer, at other times a little more planning is needed if plants are to be grown from seed. Either way, you'll love every minute of it. The only danger is that you'll run out of space!

Dwarf botanical tulips like these 'Johann Strauss' look captivating in a shallow bowl teased open by sunlight and underplanted with violets.

THINGS TO CONSIDER

Getting the right plants and containers married up for your own unique requirements is rather like shopping for a holiday destination, the decor for a room or for a new suit. You need to go through a decision-making process to be sure of getting exactly what you want. Yet it's not a chore; in fact, choosing is half the fun. Since it's invaluable to be given a whole host of ideas to inspire you, this is the exact purpose of this section of the book. Having a clear picture of what could be there on that blank canvas and the hundreds of options open to you will unlock the potential of your own plot. The decision-making process is also one of elimination: a stone trough is likely to be too heavy on a tiny balcony, a dazzling display of zinnias would fail in the shade, and planting winter heathers would be a disaster if you can't stand the colour purple.

It would be realistic, too, to consider budgets at the outset. A pair of antique lead urns could cost thousands of pounds whereas in plastic something similar could be yours for under a fiver. Fortunately, plants are adaptable enough to thrive in a vast range of container materials, shapes and sizes. Few however will survive on natural rainfall alone. Container gardening therefore does call for firm commitment to a regular routine of care and maintenance if you are to get the best from your plants. But when you consider that there is no strenuous digging or weeding in a pot – as there is in a border – it is no great hardship.

CONTAINER STYLES

You can grow almost any plant in a container and the right plant can be persuaded to grow in almost anything that holds soil, though the end result may sometimes be twee (stone boots) or even vulgar (toilets).

I also draw the line at white-emulsioned car tyres as suitable vehicles to carry a lovingly tended mobile garden. Strangely enough I find some bright coloured plastic pots as appealing as mellow, weathered stone and terracotta. Plastic urns and cauldrons can look acceptable if you are working on a shoestring budget or are worried about theft from a front garden. In the end, your choice of container comes down to what sort of house you live in, where it will be sited and to individual likes and dislikes.

However, matters of good husbandry are not open to such debate, for as well as aesthetic appeal it is important to consider how practical a container is for growing plants in. This may sound a bit illogical if it is made specifically for this purpose, but shallow bowls and urns will be suitable only for a limited range of permanent plants. Most terracotta wall pots contain such a small volume of soil that they need regular watering (perhaps twice a day) and carefully chosen plants to do well.

Some containers cost a king's ransom but increase in value, while others can be bought for next to nothing or even begged for free. Here are some novel ideas to get you thinking.

● You can draw a chair up to this outdoor fireside when summer evenings begin to get chilly. French marigolds, coleus and lantana will raise the temperature when grown in a fire basket. Line it with black plastic and put fire-blackened logs down the front to add authenticity.

● Old coppers, which are much sought-after as planters, in time develop a wonderful, blue patina. Such a big container needs bold treatment. Here, some blowsy, yellow tulips tower above blue and yellow polyanthus and trailing ivy to create a visual feast.

● Ali Baba jars add mystery – inviting visitors to peep inside – but if you do decide to add greenery choose trailers to cover the top and tumble down the sides. Plant a pot that fits snugly on the rim. Here, coils of dried seaweed have been added to the succulent sedum.

● Troughs as big as this home-made one are roomy enough for a brilliant bedding display and a climber or two at the back as a permanent fixture. The framework is made from 7.5 cm (3 in) x 5 cm (2 in) timber clad with half-round logs lined with heavy-gauge polythene.

● Painting and stencilling are popular ways to personalise a wooden container, but when it's a well-weathered, oak barrel like this one, it's a shame to cover all that natural ageing. Here, fir cones – secured to the rope with screw eyes – have been hung along the front.

● Black plastic cauldrons are roomy enough to grow three or four plants and light enough to lift up for a table display. This combination of wild pansy with *Nemesia denticulata* 'Confetti' and grey-and-white-splashed foliage is a real winner.

11

• Dark green or brown plastic urns always seem preferable to the ubiquitous, glaring white ones, and the wider and deeper they are the better your plant display will be. For a summer-long show, try a mixture of heathers, coleus and ajuga to colonise the rim.

• These imported, shallow terracotta planters are like giant pudding bowls, superb for packing in summer bedding plants, but likely to get lost at ankle height. Raise them up using an urn pedestal or a terracotta pot and they'll look as good as this one does.

• Buff slabs are the most popular choice for patios so it makes sense to pick out troughs and pots made from similarly coloured reconstituted stone or concrete. Various finishes are available such as Cotswold (like this) and a paler Bath stone.

• Leaky, pensioned-off, galvanised or enamel buckets make ideal homes for plants with a wandering root system like mint or these Chinese lanterns. However, don't be tempted to paint the surface – the weathered look is all the rage!

● Terracotta wall pots can be used in the garden in the same way as you hang up pictures to decorate the lounge, though with such limited room for soil they dry out very quickly and it may be worth considering an automatic watering system to keep them happy.

● Shallow terracotta pans are popular with bonsai growers, but they also look great pushed end to end and planted with the same bedding plant in a different colour. These snapdragons are edged with ajugas, and the pans have been stood in front of lavender.

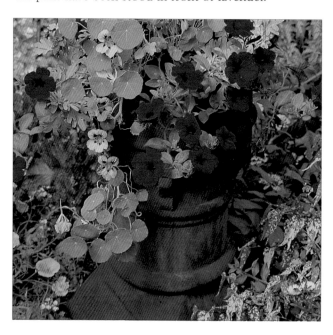

● Small woodland plants like cyclamen will thrive on an old tree stump or hollow trunk if you keep it constantly moist. Be careful, however, that the rotting wood does not introduce the dreaded, black, thread-like strands of honey fungus into your garden soil.

● Chimney pots are perhaps the tallest containers we can plant and as such are invaluable to give instant height amongst clusters of pots or at the edge of a border, as here. A pair, planted like this with trailing nasturtiums and petunias, are perfect flanking a door.

STRIKING COLOUR SCHEMES

There are plenty of ideas here to tempt you, some taking their prompt from the colour of the container or even an individual, two-tone flower.

If you've never thought of colour theming your pots, you may be surprised to know that the less you put in, the more you get out of your containers – at least as far as the number of colours is concerned – though you do need a lot of self-control to stick to just one. If you're a little unsure as to what goes with what, why not limit your ideas to two or three tried and tested colour blends: blue and yellow, pink and blue, orange and blue, and so on.

In spring you can usually get away with more outrageous colour combinations, because there is so much greenery in the garden to soften the impact. In summer there is an explosion of possibilities and the chances are you'll come up with something unique and, if you like it, who cares what others think – though I've yet to see an orange-and-magenta success story. Even in wintertime there are good pairings to be had. For example, in a container you can bring foliage and flower into such close proximity that they will often have twice the impact of the same plants in a border.

You can also select colours to suit your mood. Cool blues and white are just the thing to refresh you in the heat of the day. Alternatively, use yellow flowers to create artificial sunshine on dull days and add reds and oranges to really turn up the heat. It's great fun. Why not try it?

● Sometimes the colouring on the faces of pansies is so special that it's worth giving them a setting all of their own. These *Viola* x *wittrockiana* 'Melody Sunrise' were planted in a nest of chocolate-coloured heuchera and ajuga leaves to highlight the blooms.

● If you pick out the richest colours from the summer bedding sales benches and gather them together like this you will have a really sumptuous show. Here we have *Salvia coccinea* 'Lady in Red', red pelargoniums, yellow African marigolds and red and blue petunias.

• A coloured pot like this blue-glazed bowl is a good starting point for a special theme. The selected flowers range through palest blue (*Pulmonaria* 'Highdown') to the rich, velvety primrose (*Primula* 'Midnight') and the exquisite, silky *Crocus vernus* 'Purpureus Grandiflorus'.

• You can create some real drama in late spring by sticking to a colour scheme using yellow and maroon. The pansy was the starting point, then the yellow early double tulips and double primrose were added and, for foliage, red houseleek, grey sedum and bronze fennel.

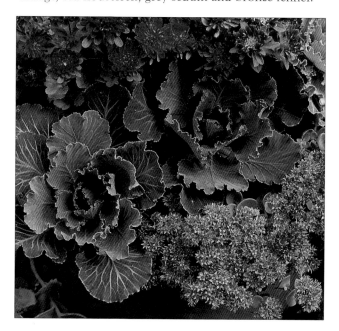

• Unusual summer annuals like these golden daisies (*Ursinia anthemoides*) or *Salvia coccinea* 'Lady in Red' are easily raised from seed. This is well worth the effort as they can rarely be bought. Mix in some silver and purple leaves for a striking colour scheme.

• It becomes progressively more difficult to make a splash towards the end of summer, but asters can always be relied upon to create colourful interest. The colour pink dominates this planter with ornamental cabbages, mixed dwarf asters and *Sedum ewersii*.

15

• A trough can become a feast of colour by alternating purple and pink winter heathers backed up by pink and blue hyacinths. To ensure they peak together, pot up your hyacinth bulbs in autumn and force them under glass or buy pot-grown bulbs once in bloom.

• These spectacular South African heathers are a great way to pep up flagging container displays before the winter heathers come into full bloom. They fit in well with blue-leaved conifers, but don't expect them to survive severe frosts unless very well protected.

• Double daisies and violets are diminutive charmers for late spring and their colours never seem to clash. This blend of pink, purple and yellow is particularly pleasing – and a great recipe for the front of a windowbox or trough.

• With their often outrageous colours, tulips can provide some of the best opportunities to conjure up a bit of plant magic. *Narcissus* 'Tricolet' here tones in beautifully with these *Tulipa* 'Garden Answers', orange wallflowers and trailing *Euphorbia myrsinites*.

● Imported glazed pots are usually frostproof and beautifully coloured. This mid-blue bowl is crammed full of spring violets and the cup-shaped daisies of *Anemone blanda*. A touch of yellow adds contrast without losing the harmony between plants and container.

● Pastel pinks and blues are soft, restful and easy on the eye. Here blue *Campanula poscharskyana* trails into a pink-flowered marguerite, over the glaucous leaves of dicentra planted below and through yellow-foliaged physocarpus growing in an adjoining pot.

● The ragged leaves of ornamental kale 'Red Peacock' have veins and midribs of a lighter purple-pink. Here, white-fringed petunias, whose flowers pick up the kale leaves to perfection, are growing up through its leaves to give a summer-long show.

● Orange flowers can be refreshing and vibrant when combined with purple and have never looked better than in this clever mixture of pansies in a reconstituted stone pot. Don't let the unpopularity of orange as a bedding-plant colour frighten you from using it.

HOT SPOTS

Plants grown in containers positioned on paving or beside a house wall are particularly vulnerable in sunny weather.

If long, hot summers and water rationing are here to stay, it therefore makes sense to choose plants that revel in such conditions. Busy lizzies and tobacco plants, for example, are not suitable as they'll need watering twice a day.

In the increasingly Mediterranean climate we are experiencing, many of our gardens are beginning to take on a rather exotic flavour, with pots brimming with daisies and architectural foliage plants. For plants that come from countries like Australia, Mexico and South Africa, it is becoming a real home from home as they have revelled in the hot sunshine.

Several tell-tale signs indicate the sort of plants that are able to withstand exposure to hot sun and periods of drought, although, when restricted in a pot, only a handful will thrive on just natural rainfall. Fat, juicy leaves (as on many succulents) are one such indicator and narrow, spiky foliage (as on yuccas, cabbage palms and grasses) is another. Hairy or grey-felted leaves (as on pelargoniums and lavender) will also reduce water loss.

Drought-busters are especially useful for colonising shallow containers that hold only small quantities of soil or for pots in inaccessible places such as on a high wall or perched on a brick pier. When you do need to water, use one of those slightly curved lances that fit on the end of a hosepipe to give you extra reach into the container.

● Carpeting thyme is well suited to drought conditions and searing heat, and three varieties that contrast in leaf and flower create a classic composition for this shallow, terracotta pan. Finish off the display with a dressing of fine chippings, and site the pan in full sun.

● The houseleeks in this shallow, cast-iron urn will survive on just rain from the heavens, though you will get much juicier rosettes if you water two or three times a week in hot weather. Add plenty of grit to the potting compost to ensure good drainage.

• Plants with a rosette of narrow, sword-like leaves will often tolerate a few days of missed watering. They also lend an exotic atmosphere to the garden, particularly when grouped like this purple cabbage palm, agave succulent and yuccas, creating a feast of foliage.

• When you've got a pelargonium as exuberant and distinctive as 'Frank Headley', it's worth giving it a special setting. This wooden planter picks up the sage-green colour in the pelargonium's white-variegated leaf and is one of a pair flanking a matching bench.

• Many members of the daisy family are real sunseekers, like these blue kingfisher daisies (*Felicea*) tumbling past a decorated terracotta pot filled with grey-leaved echeveria succulents. They make a lovely combination on top of this retaining wall.

• Zinnias are stunning in a pot all to themselves when the sun shines, but they have a reputation for sulking in wet summers. Don't sow the seed too early. Mid May is soon enough, in an unheated greenhouse or indoors on a light windowsill.

19

SHADY CORNERS

Although foliage plants are the most obvious choice for containers set in shade, a host of bedding plants like fuchsias, begonias, busy lizzies and monkey musk also relish a cool spot out of the sun's glare.

A lot of pot-grown, spring flowers such as primroses and anemones are well adapted to life in the shade of hedgerows and woodland. In summer, they just tick over or die down below soil level. Finding summer-flowering plants that tolerate shade is far more likely to be a problem. When robbed of sunlight, plants such as marigolds and geraniums produce more leaf than flower and grow tall and spindly.

It's important to be aware of the difference between shade cast by overhanging tree branches and shade from a wall or fence, where the indirect light levels will be far higher and consequently your choice of shade lovers much enhanced. A pot-grown plant will often grow better beneath a tree canopy or at the base of a wall than one planted directly in the ground, where it has to compete for water and nutrients. Some trees such as yew, however, do cast particularly heavy shade while others such as lime and sycamore may drip sticky honeydew on plants below.

Green and blue leaves generally do better in shade than variegated ones, which may revert to plain green. Some of the largest-leaved plants grow in semi-shade, where an increased surface area is needed to gather all available light, so again look to nature to point the way.

● This superb, purple-leaved Japanese maple is an ornament that any gardener would love to use to give character to a shady spot. In this particular situation, however, the leaves could be spoilt by sticky honeydew dripping from the birch canopy above.

● Fuchsias, like this 'Swingtime', will thrive at the base of a north-facing wall. Take the opportunity to build up a display that will lighten up the area, as well as conceal the bareness of the slabs and walls, by adding trailing lobelia and a yellow-leaved pig-a-back plant.

● You can make a really welcoming frontage to your home, even if it gets no sun, by maintaining a collection of potted evergreens (here *Rhododendron yakushimanum*) and Japanese maples supplemented by lush foliage plants, like hostas, that excel in containers.

● Plants such as fuchsias and busy lizzies are excellent for providing flower colour in shady areas. For an eye-catching, banked display, position them in a cluster of three pots of differing heights, fuchsias to the back and busy lizzies in the front.

● Some foliage plants are quite capable of making their mark without association with other species. The brown spring leaves of *Rodgersia podophylla* look splendid on their own in a wooden tub mulched with cobbles, and will double in size in a month.

● Ferns are amongst the first plants that spring to mind when we think of shade. A collection of three with contrasting leaf shapes makes a fine trio for clay pots, and they will grow contentedly for years as long as they are not allowed to dry out.

21

USING SPRING BULBS

Like fireworks, bulbs are ready-made surprise packages. You just plant them, stand back and wait for the show. They are tailor-made for pots and with a bit of advance planning you can double your spring colour.

Thumbing through those glossy bulb catalogues in late summer and autumn, or drooling over pre-packed wall displays at your local garden centre or nursery is like being let loose in a sweet shop. The choice is almost overwhelming and all will light up your garden from the first stirring of snowdrops and crocus in winter to the last tulips of spring. For exposed sites, it's best to avoid tall floppy daffodils and tulips, which are easily blown over. Hyacinths too may flop over the edge of the pot as they age, but that is all part of their charm.

The secret when buying bulbs is to aim for continuity so that, like a relay race, several bulbs may come into flower together, overlapping with bedding plants such as primroses and pansies. Then, as they fade, new varieties are ready to carry on the show.

If you're clever, you can manipulate your potted bulb collection to defy the seasons by bringing some into a greenhouse and holding back others in a cool shady spot outside so that for an anniversary or wedding you will have a real flower festival of your very own creation – far more satisfying (and cheaper) than buying them all in flower.

● Winter heathers are perhaps the most valuable of all types, but why be content with a sheet of pink, white or purple when you could have twice the impact by planting dwarf bulbs, like these crocus, in-between their wiry stems to make an embroidered carpet.

● Early double tulips are amongst the best choice for small to medium-sized containers. They are sturdy, compact and available in a myriad of colours. 'Fringed Beauty' is a really hot customer, especially with red and yellow wallflowers and brassy yellow, dwarf doronicums.

• You can sometimes develop a theme based on the colour of your container. This vegetable tureen is ideal to play host to scented *Iris reticulata* and white crocus, though you must water carefully as there is no drain hole, and site it out of rain to avoid waterlogging.

• Pansies really get into their stride in April and May, and De Caen anemones make lovely companions to have alongside. They are vibrant, tough and easily grown. Plant them between the pansies as dry tubers in autumn or in bud in spring from smaller pots.

• Every plant has a perfect partner and colour matching is one of the greatest joys of gardening. Try this blend of white, yellow-eyed primroses with cheeky blue *Anemone blanda* for a cool, sophisticated show. Both can be set out in a border after flowering.

• Scale is an important factor to consider with container gardening. When you plant small bulbs, like these 'Tête-à-Tête' daffodils, surround them with plants of similar stature (here crocus, crocus tulip, mixed primroses and *Veronica peduncularis* 'Georgia Blue').

23

FOLIAGE FINESSE

Foliage plants have many moods conjuring up visions of steamy jungles or dry, arid landscapes, and most will thrive in a pot.

After indulging in all that explosive outpouring of summer colour, isn't it nice to gaze out on a cool oasis of luxuriant foliage, although some yellow-leaved evergreens may provide a ray of sunshine throughout the year. Many of the larger-leaved kinds will grow to surprising proportions given a big enough container and, of course, plenty of feeding and watering.

Pot culture also enables us to grow tender exotics like bananas and coleus on the patio in summer and return them to the warmth of a conservatory, greenhouse or well-lit room before the first frosts. Their leaves will continue to give pleasure even after the most prolific flowering plant is spent.

The fun begins when you start to group together your plants so they offer maximum contrast with each other: spiky leaves with broad, rounded shapes; soft, feathery foliage with bold, jagged-edged leaves; yellow with reds, greys with purple. For real drama, site one of the extroverts, like giant rhubarb, in splendid isolation in a half barrel to make an irresistible focal point. In its second year you should be able to rest in its shade, though don't imagine that you have to grow giants to make your mark. There are some exquisite, small-leaved foliage plants amongst ferns and ornamental grasses and don't forget dual-purpose plants such as astilbes and bergenias that have handsome flowers and leaves.

● The explosion of luscious leaves in spring and early summer can be enjoyed at close quarters in pots stood on gravel. Here, deadnettles and epimedium vie for attention with the almost black-leaved *Anthriscus sylvestris* 'Ravenswing' and dwarf ornamental rhubarb.

● Even on a dull day, a yellow-leaved evergreen like this *Choisya ternata* 'Sundance' will inject a bit of artificial sunshine and really cheer you up. A member of the orange family, it has scented leaves and flowers, and needs warmth and shelter in cold areas in winter.

● For a classic foliage threesome that will succeed even in a shallow tomato tray like this, try *Hosta* 'June', *Carex oshimensis* 'Evergold' and *Houttuynia cordata* 'Chamaeleon'. Slow down the mint-like spread of the houttuynia by keeping it in its pot.

● Ornamental cabbage and kale represent some of the most exciting newcomers for seasonal bedding and are particularly bold in late summer and autumn, when cooler temperatures encourage the rich pink and purple leaves to intensify in colour.

● If you fancy a show of coloured foliage that will really leap out at you, mix together the most extrovert, yellow-variegated leaves you can find, combining three or even four shades. Perhaps the most useful plants are those that also have bold flowers.

● A collection of leafy herbs can be sited in a pot or two alongside your favourite garden seat. Run your fingers through them to release the delightful fragrance from pineapple sage, chamomile, apple mint, lad's love and lemon-scented pelargonium. Absolute bliss!

25

COUNTRY STYLE

In a garden you can deliberately go out of your way to deceive, because even if you live in a town or city it's still possible to manufacture a small piece of idyllic countryside.

Mixed hedges of thorn and hazel, wild flowers creeping in at the boundaries and apple trees weighed down with fruit go a long way towards achieving the country look. Containers, too, can play a big part – and who wouldn't want to own a small slice of the countryside, even if it is only encapsulated in a few pots? The look is achieved in two ways.

Firstly, your choice of plants is important. Cram your pots full to their brim with annuals and perennials that will shoot skywards and spill over the rim. Spiky New Zealand flax and cabbage palms will never work; they are far too exotic. Some would also rule out variegated leaves or bright yellow and sombre purple foliage and, indeed, in tree form they can jar against a backcloth of rich greens. Highly bred plants such as petunias and red salvias can also look too man-made for an authentic country look.

Secondly, look out for nicely weathered pots without elaborate decoration – simple, hand-thrown terracotta, shallow baskets and sun-bleached oak barrels. Stone troughs are also good, though the genuine article is now very expensive. There are, however, some very convincing concrete reproductions available, which are distressed to look old. Stand your pots on salvaged brick or stone flags or on increasingly sophisticated, simulated versions of these.

● This patio is a mirror image of the cottage wall behind and a great backdrop for a container show. Long-tom terracotta pots were chosen to house yellow lysimachia, sweet William and marguerites but beware on windy sites as they may blow over and crack.

● In this subtle country scheme, a pot and flaking door set the theme for a subdued mix of love-lies-bleeding and tobacco plants intricately woven through with floss flowers and brachycome. Yellow creeping jenny softens the edge of this composition.

● This brick wall makes a splendid location for a collection of cottage-garden favourites like sunflowers, hollyhocks, pansies and herbs. Don't make it all too clean and tidy. A bit of decay, a few yellow leaves and plants encroaching on each other enhance the look.

● Sun-bleached oak and rusting bands of iron add character to this wallflower display. The white brickwork and weatherboard behind throw each flower into sharp focus, and the colours and perfume of the wallflowers seem to instil the very essence of a country garden.

● Violas are highly collectable, diminutive charmers, and these rustic shelves are just the place to show them off and bring the scented varieties closer to the nose. Stack the clay pots in decreasing sizes and station your biggest plants at the base so the shelves don't look top heavy.

● Wicker log baskets filled with lavender and flowering perennials are a lovely way to welcome visitors to your front door. You don't have to plant them permanently. These lady's mantle, Canterbury bells and sweet Williams are still in their original plastic pots.

27

PERMANENT PLANTING

Some plants are so well adapted to life in a pot that they can be seen as virtually permanent fixtures and if well maintained will add character and maturity amongst more fleeting bedding plants.

Growing plants in pots is addictive and you'll soon have an ever-expanding collection in all shapes and sizes. Rather than continually changing each one with summer bedding plants followed by spring bedding and bulbs, it's a good idea to plant up some with a permanent framework of evergreens, such as conifers, rhododendrons, camellias and heathers, to clothe the patio in winter. Herbaceous plants like hostas, dicentras and hellebores with good leaves and flowers will also earn their keep from year to year amongst the more fleeting annuals.

Permanent plants don't have to be grown as isolated individuals, each in their own container. Larger pots, troughs and tubs can have two or three permanent, hardy plants around which the bedding and bulbs are set out. Alternatively, once a camellia or rhododendron has finished flowering it can be moved away from the main display area and brought out again the following year to repeat the performance.

Container-grown, permanent plants are also at a premium where surfaces such as tarmac make it impossible to plant a climber in any other way, and a pair of potted and clipped box or bay trees flanking a door is still a design classic.

● There are some exquisite varieties of dicentra that have delicate, often grey-green leaves and pendant, locket-shaped flowers that last for weeks in spring and summer. Here 'Pearl Drops' and 'Stuart Boothman' have been in pots for two years in a semi-shaded area.

● During the dead of winter, there is sometimes little but evergreens to fall back on. However, conifers of contrasting colour and form when combined with dwarf hebe, as here, can look really cheery. With a powdering of snow, you could almost be in the Alps.

• These hardy slipper flowers bloom after the two spring-flowering evergreens (rhododendron and pieris) have finished, while variegated hostas and purple-leaved bugle carry the interest forward right through summer and contrast well with the shrubs' new growth.

• Formal, square casks or Versailles tubs never look better than when planted with a clipped box spire or pyramidal conifer like this *Thuja occidentalis* 'Rheingold'. The tubs can be painted to match any patio trellis or even house colours if used as a pair to flank a doorway.

• A stone trough looks better when permanently planted with alpines or slow-growing, truly dwarf conifers (like these) – or perhaps a combination of the two – than with a riot of nasturtiums or petunias that would quickly hide its weathered surface.

• Some 'permanent' plants are less long-lived than others. After a couple of years these violets will need replacing with new ones, but the beautiful rock rose, pink heucherella and fleshy sedum should last twice as long before they need to be transferred to a border.

29

POSITIONING YOUR POTS

Now we've looked at container styles, colour schemes and ideas for sun and shade, you will probably be well on the way to composing your own display. You have a mental picture. Now what about the picture frame?

Putting your containers into an appropriate setting can double their impact. Like choosing the decor for a room, your pots are part of the garden furnishings and it's important that they don't strike a discordant note. Simple, hand-thrown, weathered terracotta pots demand a suitably modest setting. Ornate urns and classically decorated pots lend themselves to more formal treatment spaced perhaps equidistantly along a balustrade or straight pathway, or limited to just one imposing planter set up on a pedestal. It's also important to consider scale as well as style. Small pots can be swallowed up and lost in the open garden whereas, when grouped together, they not only catch the eye but are also easier to maintain.

Positioned on stark expanses of paving or brickwork, it's hardly surprising that many containers fail to realise their potential. Far better to site a random assortment of containers as individuals enveloped in planting, raised up just enough to show off the top half of the container or in a sea of gravel where carpeting alpines and herbs can spread freely around the base. You do however need easy access for what is often daily maintenance.

● These pots of French marigolds stand out from the crowd and frustrate the attentions of slugs and snails by resting on pedestals made from clay chimney liners and upturned pots. Even a terracotta rhubarb forcer will provide a good perch in summer.

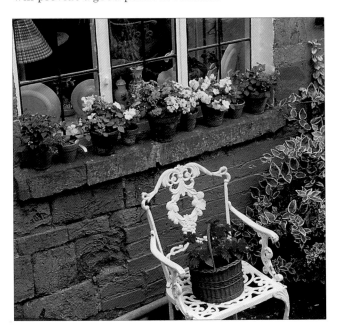

● As an alternative to a conventional windowbox, a parade of small pots lined up on a windowsill and planted with pansies or busy lizzies looks charming from inside and out. Aim for uniformity and select pots of the same size and shape.

● As an inexpensive and eye-catching way to flatter a large container, eight bricks can be laid like the spokes of a wheel on a bed of gravel. In time, the pansies will seed into the gravel. If you're impatient, why not plant some pansies amongst the fragrant creeping thyme.

● Stone troughs like this are usually planted with alpines and stood on four bricks on the patio, but this one has been ingeniously built into a stone, retaining wall. The profusion of lady's mantle and the greenery 'anchors' it to the spot.

● Against colour-washed walls it is always tempting to develop a Mediterranean theme. Props like this tall honeycomb jar add to the atmosphere, as do lavender, scented-leaved lemon verbena, fleshy agave, yellow marguerites and the red bottlebrush flowers.

● A roomy, wooden wheelbarrow makes a picturesque home for a cluster of pots filled with early spring flowers and buds. Being mobile, it can be sited around a doorway or even under the house windows for armchair viewing. The pots are insulated with straw.

31

• A bold group of three large pots of similar shape but contrasting sizes makes more impact than 30 tiny ones scattered at random over the patio. These blue-glazed Chinese pots were planted with a permanent framework of evergreens supplemented by seasonal bedding.

• A bare wall can be almost instantly turned into a feature by the clever use of wall pots. Group them together for maximum impact, avoid straight lines and don't forget to include a comfy seat where you can sit back amid your handiwork.

• A flight of steps make a wonderful, tiered stage setting for pots, provided they are built wide enough to allow the edges to be decorated. Machine-rounded logs (for risers) and granite setts (for treads) are ideal materials for making curved steps.

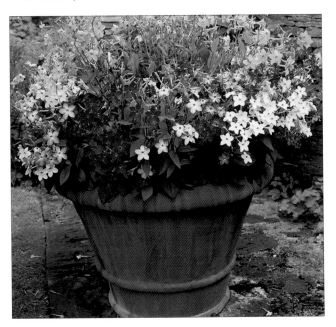

• An outsized container like this has enough presence to stand in splendid isolation as a centrepiece in a courtyard or at the end of a vista. The planting should be equally bold and stick exclusively to one species, like these superb tobacco plants.

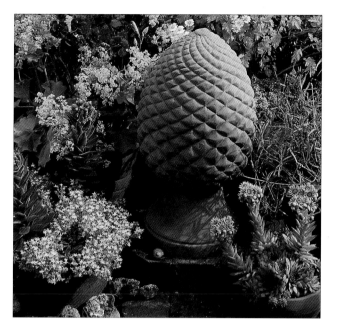

● This trio of pots planted with succulents and succulent-leaved alpines sits on a plinth of Yorkstone and pebble paving retained by a brick edge. It forms a small terraced area overlooked from the house and successfully highlights this collection of special pots.

● Occasionally a cluster of pots needs a little extra something to give it a lift. This stylish terracotta pineapple provides just such an irresistible focal point amongst cottage-garden favourites like lady's mantle, pinks, lavender, golden feverfew and houseleeks.

● This handsome terracotta urn is one of a pair guarding a flight of steps – a classic arrangement that rarely fails to please. For a more dramatic contrast with the billowing, shrubby potentilla, use purple-leaved cabbage palms in the urns.

● An edging of pebbles gives this collection of busy lizzies, coleus, echeverias and pelargoniums an informal, country appeal. You could also run the pebbles as a mulch around each pot to hold them steady and visually anchor them to the ground.

THEMES AND SCHEMES

If you're the sort of cook who dreams up delicious meals without any prompting then there's a good chance that this creative flair will overflow into the garden and your pots will be brimming with your own unique recipes, too. Most of us, however, need to smell the sizzle and see the prize before we enter the affray, so in this section I've done all the work for you. I've planned, grown and photographed more than 30 of my favourite planting schemes, which encompass a whole host of containers, plants and seasons. Some are effortlessly achieved; it's hard to fail with cosmos and petunias (pages 60–61), even if you're growing them from seed for the first time. Others, such as the Cottage Pot (pages 62–63), are more of a challenge, though the rewards are greater – and won't your friends be impressed when you say 'all my own work'. To encourage you on your way, there are simple, illustrated instructions for planting up a container on pages 100–101.

Nor need there be a dull moment in your mobile garden. As soon as one plant or scheme goes over, the secret is to have replacements waiting in the wings. There are plenty of ideas here to keep the pot boiling and indications of how long each show will continue. Among the schemes are ones to warm you up in the dead of winter (including Christmas itself), to scent the air, to fill your salad bowl or to cool you down on a hot day. Why don't you try one for each season of the year. I'm sure you'll be back for more!

Hyacinth Parade

Compared to the poise and elegance of a dwarf daffodil or tiny wild cyclamen, a hyacinth can come across as a bit of a clumsy heavyweight. It has a stiff rigidity that would strike a discordant note naturalised in grass for example. I don't care a bit, because in many of the best garden plantings an understanding of a plant's personality is the key to its success. A hyacinth excels in a formal setting so I lined up these 'China Pink' at the back of a stoneware trough. With crocus and 'Wanda' hybrid primroses they looked rich and regal and their intoxicating perfume wafted on the slightest breeze. Although not quite as free flowering as the florists' varieties, 'Wanda' hybrid primroses are hardier and make better garden plants. Their leaves are often tinged with purple.

YOU WILL NEED

a reconstituted-stone trough, 43 cm (17 in) x 20 cm (8 in), finished in Cotswold colour
6 pink hyacinths (*Hyacinthus* 'China Pink')
20 crocus (*C. vernus* 'Purpureus Grandiflorus') · 5 mixed hybrid primroses (*Primula* 'Wanda')

PERIOD OF INTEREST
March and April

LOCATION
In sun or shade near an open window or doorway.

FOR CONTINUITY
Plant out the crocus and hyacinths in the garden and replace them with pansies and forget-me-nots.

Plant up the hyacinths and crocus in autumn and transfer them to your trough in spring. Alternatively you can buy pot-grown hyacinths and crocus in bloom in spring. I forced on my pink hyacinths under glass so they were in bloom with the crocus. Fill the trough to one-third with compost. Arrange the hyacinths at the back. Then plant the crocus and primroses. Top up with compost and water in.

GOOD ADVICE
● Think carefully about where you position your trough and get someone to help lift it in place before you fill it.
● Make way for a summer display by planting out the primroses amongst snakeshead fritillaries and cowslips in a semi-shaded spot.

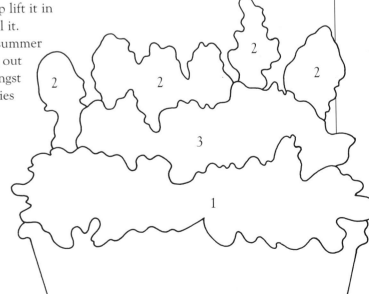

1 *hybrid primroses*
2 *hyacinths*
3 *crocus*

Double Delight

I have always retained a child-like fascination for members of the daisy family. They have an innocence and simplicity about them even when the petals are increased a hundred fold to make a fully double bloom like these spring bedding daisies. Too lavish a container would intimidate them so I chose a weathered garden riddle to show them off. With the ever-increasing use of soil-less composts, however, these sieves are more likely to be seen as ornaments than as an essential piece of gardening kit. They are still made today, or you can beg an old one. Deep-rooted plants like wallflowers would fail to thrive in such a shallow receptacle but fibrous-rooted daisies love it – and you don't even need to buy them as pot-grown plants. If you sow seed in summer and bed them out in a garden border, they will transplant successfully into a container the following spring.

YOU WILL NEED
a garden riddle or punctured, old, enamel washing-up bowl · plastic liner · 10 mixed double daisies (*Bellis perennis*)

PERIOD OF INTEREST
March to May

LOCATION
In sun or shade, set the riddle on bricks or granite setts, in front of a clump of bluebells or a haze of forget-me-nots.

FOR CONTINUITY
Let some seedheads self-sow around the garden and even in the lawn.

1 Slit open an old compost bag to line the riddle and add a shallow layer of potting compost. With a trowel, lift your daisies from the border with a good rootball.

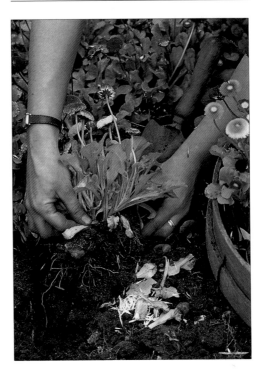

2 Before you replant them, clean up each plant by pulling off dead and yellowing leaves or dead flower stems. Pack them in the riddle tightly and fill in with more compost. Then give them a good soaking to settle them.

GOOD ADVICE
• For a finishing touch, a ring of shells makes a nice nursery-rhyme addition to hide the soil around the edge.
• Instead of raising new double daisies each year, you could transplant them from the riddle into a piece of spare ground after flowering, having split them up. Spray with an insecticide if greenfly appear on the leaves. In autumn transplant them again into borders or pots.
• Alternatively, in summer lay down the double daisies where you want them to seed, cover the roots with soil and young seedlings should appear in a few weeks' time.
• Treat forget-me-nots in the same way as double daisies for a never-ending supply, though the resulting stock may be inferior to the originals.

Spring Medley

I don't mind admitting that I'm a pansy addict. I never tire of their cheeky, impish faces. With other familiar spring personalities like forget-me-nots, grape hyacinths and double daisies they exude the sort of charm not always found in more highly bred plants. These pansies were grown from seed sown in July and overwintered in a cold frame. The grape hyacinths were potted in autumn, but there is no reason why you can't buy them in spring, pot grown and coming into bloom, though it's not quite as satisfying. The proportions look better if you group your spring medley in a shallow container rather than a deep barrel or terracotta pot. A woven basket gives a lovely informal touch to a display that meshes together to form a seductive tapestry of colour.

YOU WILL NEED
a sturdy wicker basket, 40 cm (16 in) in diameter and 20 cm (8 in) deep · plastic liner · 3 double daisies (*Bellis perennis*) 6 pansies (*Viola* x *wittrockiana* 'Gold Princess' and *V.* x *w.* 'Lilac Cap') 12 grape hyacinths (*Muscari*) · 4 dwarf forget-me-nots (*Myosotis*)

PERIOD OF INTEREST
April and May

LOCATION
In sun, on a log pile, balcony or patio table or in a porch or conservatory.

FOR CONTINUITY
Frame the pansies with 5 Junior petunias (*Petunia*, Fantasy Series, Milliflora Group).

---

1 Line the basket with black plastic, then pierce drainage holes in the liner. Add a layer of potting compost before laying out the plants.

2 Spend some time getting the plants into a pleasing arrangement, daisies to the front, pansies and grape hyacinths in the middle, forget-me-nots mainly at the back.

3 Fill in with more potting compost, taking care not to soil the blooms, then water the plants well. Gently dress the arrangement, lifting up the flowers and draping some grape hyacinths over the edge of the basket.

GOOD ADVICE
● Deadhead, water and feed regularly so the arrangement lasts all summer.
● Transplant the daisies and grape hyacinths to a border after flowering.

1 *double daisies*
2 *pansies 'Gold Princess'*
3 *pansies 'Lilac Cap'*
4 *grape hyacinths*
5 *dwarf forget-me-nots*

Basket Weave

Hay baskets have all the advantages of hanging baskets, such as instant colour where you want it, but are less prone to drying out and give a greater volume of planting. To avoid a hay basket lying empty throughout winter, with its metalwork exposed like a skeletal rib cage, strip out the remnants of your summer bedding in autumn, top up with potting compost and plant the daffodil bulbs. Alternatively for a more instant effect, wait until late February when pot-grown bulbs and spring bedding are available in flower and plant in one smooth operation. I wound in yellow weeping willow stems between the framework to help retain the moss and pick up the yellow theme above.

YOU WILL NEED
a cast-iron or plastic-coated-steel hay basket, 90 cm (36 in) x 28 cm (11 in) plastic liner · moss · prunings from weeping willow (*Salix babylonica*) or yellow-stemmed dogwood (*Cornus stolonifera* 'Flaviramea') · 9 pink and yellow polyanthus (*Primula*) · 20 daffodils (*Narcissus* 'Tête-à-Tête')

PERIOD OF INTEREST
March and April

LOCATION
Shelter is more important than sun as daffodils and polyanthus tolerate shade.

FOR CONTINUITY
Add winter heathers (*Erica*), which will flower before and after the daffodils. Replace the daffodils with buttercups (*Ranunculus asiaticus* 'Accolade').

1 Cut to size your prunings from the weeping willow or dogwood and weave them into the hay basket. Then line the back of the basket with black plastic to keep the compost away from any brickwork.

2 Fill in from behind with tightly packed sphagnum moss – or you could even take some from your own lawn, though don't be surprised if a few weeds appear in the basket later on.

3 Add some potting compost and lay out the polyanthus and daffodils while still in their pots until you have a pleasing arrangement. Tap off the pots, insert the plants into the compost and water well.

GOOD ADVICE
• Push some small-leaved, variegated ivies (*Hedera*) through the moss and willow-stem layer if you want to fill out the front of the basket. These can be retained for summer.
• Plant the daffodils in a border after flowering.

1 *weeping willow stems*
2 *polyanthus*
3 *daffodils*

Mellow Yellow

Overdosing on undiluted yellow flowers – such as forsythia in spring – can make your eyes water. However, as is often the case when colour scheming, a combination of yellow flowers and more soothing, yellow foliage can give a very pleasing display. Add a touch of purple and lime-green in the form of the purple-leaved wood spurge and you have a creation that generates its own sunlight with a very long season of interest. Spurges are among the most useful plants for pots, because they look good for months on end. *Euonymus fortunei* 'Emerald 'n' Gold' also earns its keep throughout the year, although it is at its most colourful as the fresh, new growth flushes in late spring.

YOU WILL NEED

a salt-glazed pot, 40 cm (16 in) in diameter
1 or 2 *Euonymus fortunei* 'Emerald 'n' Gold'
1 purple-leaved wood spurge (*Euphorbia amygdaloides* 'Purpurea') · 1 golden-leaved feverfew (*Tanecetum parthenium*)
2 or 3 black and yellow pansies (*Viola* x *wittrockiana*) · 2 *Helichrysum petiolare* 'Limelight'

PERIOD OF INTEREST
April to June

LOCATION
In sun or shade, though some sunshine will bring out the best leaf colours.

FOR CONTINUITY
Add dwarf tulips amongst the euonymus for April interest and African or French, yellow or vanilla marigolds as a replacement for the spurge in late May.

1 Assemble your chosen plants, including one good-sized or two smaller euonymus plants, and water them all well. Then fill the pot with potting compost to within 5–7.5 cm (2–3 in) of the rim. Plant the centre of the pot with the euonymus.

2 Add the wood spurge. Carefully tuck in the feverfew and pansies amongst the euonymus. Top up the compost and give it a good soaking. Wait until early May before adding the helichrysum.

GOOD ADVICE
● You may find feverfew seedlings in your own or a friend's garden.
● To avoid powdery mildew, spray the wood spurge with a fungicide every 10–14 days.
● Transfer the wood spurge to a border in late May.

1 *euonymus*
2 *wood spurge*
3 *feverfew*
4 *pansies*
5 *helichrysum*

Wedgwood

A special container calls for a special planting theme and I was rather taken with this lion's head trough. It was deep enough to take a specimen-sized pieris, which I had been growing in a pot for two years, with room around the front for more seasonal plants. I gathered up some crocus, hyacinths and double primroses, and soon the blue-and-white theme had become inescapable. Such a colour scheme always looks cool and sophisticated and is quite a contrast to all those unplanned explosions of mixed spring colours you can get if you don't buy your plants in selected shades. As well as the plant range seen here, you can get your blues and whites from *Anemone blanda*, pansies, violets and grape hyacinths, so there are plenty of variations on this theme.

YOU WILL NEED

a reconstituted-stone or plastic trough, 55 cm (22 in) x 40 cm (16 in) · ericaceous potting compost · 2 double blue primroses (*Primula* 'Blue Sapphire') · 1 *Pieris japonica* 'Cupido' · 5 blue and 5 white hyacinths 10 white crocus

PERIOD OF INTEREST
March to early May

LOCATION
In sun or shade, on paving near a window and door or by a garden path where the hyacinths' scent can be enjoyed.

FOR CONTINUITY
Add dwarf *Iris reticulata*, which will flower before the crocus.

1 You can plant up the trough in autumn, buy plants in flower in spring, or copy me and pot up your bulbs in autumn and transfer them to the trough in April. Arrange the potted plants into a pleasing display.

2 Clean up the primroses by picking off any yellow or decaying leaves and spent flowers. Also remove any slugs!

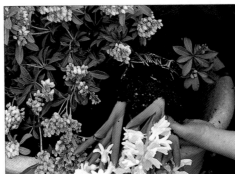

3 Add a thick layer of potting compost to the trough and plant the pieris at the back. Then add the hyacinths and lastly the crocus and primroses. Fill in any gaps with compost and water in.

GOOD ADVICE
• Use a lime-free, ericaceous potting compost to prevent the pieris turning yellow.
• After flowering, return the pieris to its original pot. Plant the other plants in the border.

1 *double primroses*
2 *pieris*
3 *hyacinths*
4 *crocus*

Summer Magic

Container gardening is addictive and the deeper you become immersed in the hobby the more success you'll enjoy. In no time at all you'll find you want to take on new challenges, and this usually means propagating your own plants from seed and cuttings. If you're a new recruit, this recipe of Junior petunias and dwarf coneflowers is easily achieved by buying in young plants in May and June. By late July you'll be revelling in a sea of blooms. Alternatively, if that's too easy or you want more for your money, both plants can be raised from seed sown in March in a heated propagator or on a windowsill indoors. Whichever way you choose, don't bury the plants too deeply in their display container nor overfirm the compost, or they will suffer through lack of air at the roots.

YOU WILL NEED
an oval or rectangular, terracotta trough, 40 cm (16 in) x 20 cm (8 in) · 3 dwarf coneflowers (*Rudbeckia hirta* 'Becky Mxd') 3 Junior petunias (*P.*, Fantasy Series, Milliflora Group)

PERIOD OF INTEREST
June to September

LOCATION
In full sun. Why not stand the trough on the edge of a border with other daisies planted behind it.

FOR CONTINUITY
Pinch off the spent petunia flowers, so they don't set seed. The coneflowers need only occasional deadheading.

1 Cover the drainage hole with broken crocks or, if these are difficult to obtain, a flat piece of polystyrene. Add more broken up polystyrene in the base. This will save potting compost, particularly in a deep pot.

2 If heavy, move the pot into its display area before filling it with potting compost to within 2.5 cm (1 in) of the rim. Gently tease apart any plants (such as the coneflowers here) that have been grown in a seed tray.

3 Pick off any broken or yellow leaves. Plant the coneflowers, then add the petunias along the front. Top up the compost if necessary, then tap the trough once or twice to settle the compost. Finally, water well with a fine rose.

GOOD ADVICE
• If you are planting up a brand-new, terracotta pot, immerse it in water overnight to prevent the clay pot drawing out excess moisture from the potting compost.
• Add water-retaining gel to the potting compost if you want to cut down on watering.

1 *coneflowers*
2 *petunias*

Summer Pastels

Soft colours will always be in demand when a delicate touch is called for in the garden, though it's not often that such colours are found in a packet of seeds sold as a mixture rather than separate individual colours. *Nemesia* 'Tapestry' (syn. *N.* 'Pastel') includes a scrumptious range of bicolours, pale yellows, golds, faded pinks and purples and is quite capable of making a feature on its own. It is simplicity itself to grow from seed sown in April and is quickly into flower. However, as bedding plants go, it is at its best for weeks rather than months, so I like to plant it behind a more permanent edging such as these grey-leaved senecios and brachycome daisies, which give some substance to the container when the nemesia has gone over. I thought the mellow, grey trough was the perfect foil for the flowers and its medieval carving linked in rather well with the general tapestry theme of the nemesia.

1 Half fill the trough with potting compost. Space out and plant up the edging, alternating the brachyscome daisies with the grey-leaved senecios. Angle the daisies slightly forward over the edge.

2 Split the nemesia into big chunks to drop in behind the edging plants. Such an unconventional transplanting method is far better than splitting a trayful of nemesia into individual plants.

3 Carefully set the nemesia chunks in position in the trough. Fill in any gaps with more potting compost. Then water the plants well to settle them in.

YOU WILL NEED
a concrete trough, 45 cm (18 in) x 23 cm (9 in) · 2 *Brachycome* 'Pink Mist' 3 *Senecio cineraria* · 24 *Nemesia* 'Tapestry'

PERIOD OF INTEREST
June and July

LOCATION
In full sun. Troughs look better on feet, raised up off the ground.

FOR CONTINUITY
Replace the nemesia with four pot-grown *Dianthus chinensis* 'Strawberry Parfait'.

GOOD ADVICE
• Sow nemesia at intervals of 2–3 weeks to get a succession of blooms throughout summer.
• Overwinter the grey-leaved senecio in a sheltered spot outdoors or move it into an unheated greenhouse.

1 *brachycomes*
2 *senecios*
3 *nemesia*

Gracious Herbaceous

In the early summer rush to select plants for containers, it is easy to have tunnel vision and consider just bedding plants. However, herbaceous plants can prove an attractive alternative. This gathering is full of character and has more variation in growth habit than a pot of, say, red salvias, French marigolds and busy lizzies. Herbaceous plants will give an almost instant effect when pot-grown, because many will have achieved their full height (if not spread) when you buy them. You can also enjoy them at close quarters in a pot while in season, and later plant them out permanently in a border to get bigger and better each year.

YOU WILL NEED

a terracotta pot, 45 cm (18 in) in diameter
1 red valerian (*Centranthus ruber* var. *coccineus*) · 2 *Salvia x sylvestris* 'Mainacht' ('May Night') · 1 *Heuchera micrantha* 'Palace Purple' · 2 cranesbill (*Geranium cinereum* 'Ballerina')

PERIOD OF INTEREST
May to August

LOCATION
In full sun on a patio. Add other pots around the base to build up the display.

FOR CONTINUITY
Dig out the salvia and valerian in July after flowering, add fresh compost and fill in with Japanese anemones (*Anemone x hybrida*) and *Rudbeckia fulgida* var *sullivantii* 'Goldsturm'.

1 Select your herbaceous plants from the wide variety available in pots in early summer. Mix flowers with coloured foliage for a balanced display.

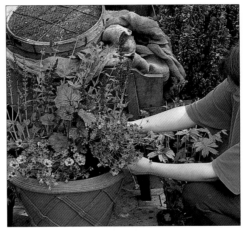

2 Half fill the pot with potting compost and plant the taller plants – the valerian and salvia – in the back. Then put the heuchera in the centre and finally slip the cranesbill in the front so it can spill over the sides. Top up the compost and firm gently, then water the plants to settle them in.

GOOD ADVICE
● When you buy plants, look for a really full pot. If you plant up your pot in April, you may be able to split a single plant into two or even three separate pieces – a real bargain.

1 valerian
2 salvia
3 heuchera
4 cranesbill

Evening Shadows

Busy lizzies are certainly amongst the most obliging of summer bedding plants. They thrive in sun and shade and flower themselves silly without the need for deadheading or pinching out, but there are times when they can be a little – well how can I put this – boring. With this is mind, I cast a critical eye over John Betteley's plans for his handsome, simulated-stone urn and suggested that he consider adding a touch of drama in the form of some black pansies that I just happened to have in the back of the car. To set these off, we planted yellow-leaved creeping Jenny to drape over the front edge. By mid-summer the display had filled out beautifully. This project proved to be a useful exercise in choosing plants to suit certain conditions (in this case, semi-shade) as well as for their colour.

YOU WILL NEED
a simulated-stone urn, 40 cm (16 in) in diameter · 3 black pansies (*Viola* x *wittrockiana*) · 2 yellow-leaved creeping Jenny (*Lysimachia nummularia* 'Aurea') 1 diascia · 5 busy lizzies (*Impatiens*)

PERIOD OF INTEREST
June to September

LOCATION
In sun, shade or semi-shade. Lift your urn on to a pedestal for greatest impact.

FOR CONTINUITY
Deadhead the pansies twice a week. If they get straggly, cut them back hard and they will bush out again from the base.

1 Pot-grown pansies frequently have a tight mat of roots woven around the base and sides of the rootball. Although it seems drastic, pull off this mat to encourage the plant to grow away rapidly after replanting.

2 Tidy up the pansies by removing any yellow and spotted leaves, faded flowers and seed pods. Fill the urn with potting compost to within 5–7.5 cm (2–3 in) of the rim.

3 While still in their pots, arrange the display, placing the creeping Jenny at the front, then the pansies, backed by the diascia and busy lizzies. Plant them in the compost, topping it up if needed, and then water them in.

GOOD ADVICE
• Give a shallow urn like this plenty of water and fertiliser if it is planted as densely as this one.
• Position your urn where it can be seen and enjoyed from the house windows.

1 *pansies*
2 *creeping Jenny*
3 *diascia*
4 *busy lizzies*

Hosta Power

If I were to list my top ten plants for container gardening, hostas – or plantain lilies – would be one of the first I'd think of. They have impeccable credentials: as well as having handsome foliage (and spikes of trumpet-shaped flowers), they will grow for years in a decent-sized pot in sun or shade. Their main drawback is that they attract slugs and snails, though growing hostas in a pot significantly reduces damage. Pick off any culprits in the evening as they emerge from each hosta's crown.

With such a symmetrically shaped plant, the usual approach is to give each variety a pot of its own and group the pots together. However, mixing and matching plants is half the fun, so I picked out two of the most spectacular and diverse hosta types and contrasted their habit with a trailing campanula.

YOU WILL NEED
a terracotta pot, 50 cm (20 in) in diameter
1 blue-leaved hosta (*H. sieboldiana* var. *elegans*) · 2 variegated hostas (*H.* 'Ground Master') · 1 *Campanula poscharskyana*

PERIOD OF INTEREST
May to October

LOCATION
In sun or shade. Sit on paving around a pond or other water feature.

FOR CONTINUITY
Plant spring bulbs like dwarf daffodils to flower before the hosta leaves emerge. Leave the old, dried flower spikes on in winter. They look quite sculptural.

Pick out hostas with several shoots growing up in the pot so you can get a really good-sized spread of leaves. Almost fill the pot with the potting compost. Plant the blue-leaved hosta at the back as it's the most vigorous. Then add the variegated hostas and campanula and water well.

GOOD ADVICE
• Pull away old campanula stems after the flowers have faded.
• Some gardeners smear grease around the pot rim to deter slugs and snails.
• Some thinner-leaved, variegated hostas can scorch in intense sunlight or shrivel if too dry, so site them in shade.

1 *blue-leaved hosta*
2 *variegated hosta*
3 *campanula*

Dapper Dahlias

Have you noticed that dahlias are rapidly shrinking? This is not such good news if you're after a great armful of blooms for harvest festival, but is great for adventurous container gardeners who want to enjoy these sparkling extroverts en masse and in a confined space. Long, narrow, terracotta troughs, as used here, do not hold that much potting compost, so you need to choose your plants carefully: African marigolds, for example, would quickly grow top-heavy and starve in such a container. My choice of dahlias here was tailored to form a back row, with the fluffy, powder-puff flowers of ageratum in front, bordered by bush lobelia. The lobelia helps to soothe and smooth over any potential colour clashes from the dahlias behind, which is just as well because they are sold in mixed colours and you can't always see what's coming!

YOU WILL NEED
a terracotta trough, 60 cm (24in) x 20 cm (8 in) · 4 dahliettas or other similar dwarf varieties that do not exceed 30 cm (12 in) · 2 floss flowers (*Ageratum*) · 3 bush lobelia (*L. erinus* 'Crystal Palace')

PERIOD OF INTEREST
June to September

LOCATION
In sun, on a recessed windowsill or low wall or on a balcony or patio.

FOR CONTINUITY
Deadhead the dahliettas twice a week.

1 Either grow your plants from seed sown in February or, as I did, buy them from a nursery or garden centre in late May or early June. Check heights and colour range on the label before you buy.

2 Fill your trough three-quarters full with potting compost. Space out the dahliettas evenly along the back and plant them. Then plant the floss flowers and lobelia, alternating them at the front of the container.

3 Tap down the trough a couple of times to settle the compost, before watering in the new plants. Then sit back and look forward to a bumper display!

GOOD ADVICE
● Dahliettas tend to flower in flushes rather than continuously, so keep them well watered and fed to encourage the next instalment.

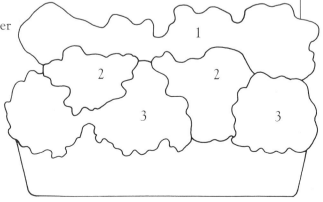

1 *dahliettas*
2 *floss flowers*
3 *lobelia*

Dynamic Duo

Virtually every plant has a perfect partner and, when you've found it, you get a great sense of achievement and an urge to share the idea. Well my dynamic duo is cosmos and petunias. The choice of cosmos is however vital: most would be far too tall and quickly shade out an underplanting so you have to stick to dwarf varieties, and 'Sonata Mxd' is the best I've grown. It is so eye-catching that it's being increasingly sold as a pot-grown bedding plant alongside more familiar favourites like begonias, lobelia and ageratum. However, it's easy to raise from seed and you can have ten times as many plants for a fraction of the price. Raising petunias from seed requires more heat and they're slower growing, so – as I did – you might decide to buy these, in which case pick out any pinks and purples that match the cosmos.

YOU WILL NEED
a wicker basket, 50 cm (20 in) in diameter
polypropylene or plastic liner
polystyrene chunks · 5 cosmos
(C. bipinnatus 'Sonata Mxd') · 5 petunias
(P. 'Celebrity Ovation') · hay

PERIOD OF INTEREST
June to September

LOCATION
In a sunny spot. A background of greenery will highlight the blooms.

FOR CONTINUITY
Cut off spent cosmos flowers before they set seed and pinch off fading petunias. Liquid feeding will prolong the show.

---

1 Sow your cosmos seed in April in a greenhouse or indoors on a windowsill. You don't need artificial heat. After two weeks prick out into cell trays, three seedlings to a cell.

2 When the cosmos plants are about 15 cm (6 in) tall, transfer them to larger pots or straight into your display basket (see below) to grow on.

3 Plant up your basket in early June. Line it first, pack out the base with the polystyrene chunks, then add the potting compost and plants. To create a country flavour, tuck in an edging of hay. Then water well.

GOOD ADVICE
• When buying petunias, look for bushy plants with dark green leaves.
• Petunias dislike heavy rain so site your basket where it will get some protection under a house wall or an open veranda.

1 cosmos
2 petunias

Cottage Pot

To me, the cottage-garden style is typified by a profusion of modest flowers growing together in one great tumbling mass without any conscious attempt at colour theming, separating roses from hardy perennials, vegetables and fruit, or keeping plants rigidly within bounds. I have here recreated just such a look by using hardy perennials (lady's mantle and cottage pinks), a tender perennial (osteospermum), a hardy annual (cornflower) and a half-hardy annual (floss flower). By starting with a suitable 'weaver' at the front of the pot – like this greeny yellow lady's mantle – you can end up with a glorious sea of intermingled colour as the 'weaver' threads itself through the other plants and then comes into flower.

YOU WILL NEED
a terracotta pot, 40 cm (16 in) in diameter
1 lady's mantle (*Alchemilla mollis*)
6 dwarf blue cornflowers (*Centaurea cyanus* 'Jubilee Gem') · 1 purple osteospermum (O. 'Sunny Lady') · 5 red cottage pinks (*Dianthus* x *allwoodii* 'Cheryl')
2 purple floss flowers (*Ageratum*)

PERIOD OF INTEREST
June to August

LOCATION
A sunny, sheltered spot will encourage flower production.

FOR CONTINUITY
Strip out the pot, retaining the floss flowers and osteospermum, top up with fresh compost and plant pot-grown asters or coneflowers.

1 Dig up a crown of lady's mantle from yours or a friend's border in March and pot it up, or buy one in May. Grow the cornflowers from seed in April; they are the only ingredients that you're unlikely to be able to buy.

2 Assemble the plants and water them well. Fill the pot with potting compost to within 5 cm (2 in) of the rim.

3 Plant the lady's mantle towards the front, backed by the osteospermum. Work the cornflowers and cottage pinks into the gaps. Add the floss flowers. Water well.

GOOD ADVICE
● For a range of cornflower colours, try *Centaurea cyanus* 'Polka Dot Mxd'.
● Spend some time 'dressing' the pot as it matures, spacing out the blooms almost as if it were a flower arrangement.

1 *lady's mantle*
2 *cornflowers*
3 *osteospermum*
4 *cottage pinks*
5 *floss flowers*

A Class Act

I'm not a plant snob, but I do like to gather around me a handful of the most refined and sophisticated plants in the same way that wine buffs stock their cellar with the finest vintages. At the top of my list must come tuberous lilies for they are beguilingly beautiful and – as luck would have it – they perform very well in containers of all shapes and sizes, even small ones like this terracotta trough. The secret to a successful display is to match the vigour of your lilies to the size of the container and its companions; then think up a subtle (or dazzling) colour scheme and you're almost there. The last factor to consider is whether the plants will be in sun or shade. My combination of lilies, an exquisite fern and double busy lizzies will be happier in shade or semi-shade than full sun, and they'll last longer too.

YOU WILL NEED

a decorated, terracotta trough, 50 cm (20 in) x 25 cm (10 in) · 5 red or pink dwarf lilies (*Lilium* 'Mr Edd') · 2 double red busy lizzies (*Impatiens*) · 1 painted fern (*Athyrium niponicum* var. *pictum*)

PERIOD OF INTEREST
June to September

LOCATION
In semi-shade near the house or a seat where you can enjoy the lilies' delicious scent.

FOR CONTINUITY
Replace the lilies after they have flowered with three pot-grown fuchsias.

---

1 Lilies in garden centres are usually sold just coming into bloom, but if you want to be sure of a specific variety and save money, pot up your own tubers in March and April and grow them on outdoors under a warm wall.

2 Gather your plants together. You can buy larger busy lizzies than these, and well in bloom, but these are typical of starter plants bought in April, potted up and grown on for 3–4 weeks.

3 Fill the trough three-quarters full with potting compost. Plant the fern first, handling its brittle fronds with care. Add the lilies along the back, then the busy lizzies. Top up the compost and water well using a fine rose.

GOOD ADVICE

● After flowering, plant out the lilies in a border with their roots in shade and their heads in sun.
● For a succession of lily blooms, pot up the tubers every 2–3 weeks.
● Busy lizzies are very tender so don't plant them out until early to mid-June.

1 *lilies*
2 *busy lizzies*
3 *painted fern*

Blazeaway Begonias

'Non Stop' begonias are aptly named. They never give up for a moment though their flowers don't get anywhere near the size of those dinner-plate blooms you see at flower shows, which need crutches and splints to hold them up. 'Non Stop' begonias are highly sociable and can be mixed with other summer flowers like busy lizzies, fuchsias and trailing lobelia that share a love of shade (though they will also perform well in full sun if well watered).

For a really eye-popping show, why not give these begonias a container to call their own. Being slightly pendulous, they will spill forwards and help to soften the edge of the tub, which, if it is decorated on the front like this one, need not be hidden beneath a cascade of trailers. As with busy lizzies, it's well worth picking off spent blooms and petals to keep the plants shipshape.

YOU WILL NEED
a reconstituted-stone planter, 38 cm (15 in) square · 5 *Begonia* 'Non Stop' in mixed colours

---

PERIOD OF INTEREST
June to September

LOCATION
In sun or shade. Plant up more 'Non Stop' begonias in a bed adjacent to your pot to create a cascade and river of colour.

FOR CONTINUITY
Don't let the begonias dry out and apply a liquid feed every 7–10 days.

---

1 Pot up your begonia corms in spring, setting them just below the compost surface, hollow side up. Grow on indoors on a windowsill or in a heated greenhouse. At first, water sparingly and not directly on to the corm.

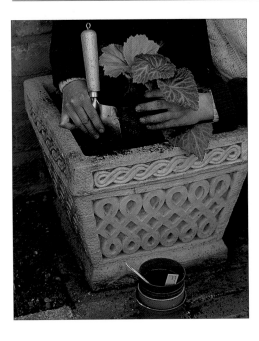

2 Once there is little danger of frosts (usually by early June), gradually harden off the plants by standing them outside against a warm wall; return them indoors if cold nights are forecast. Then almost fill the planter with potting compost and transplant the begonias, placing one plant in the centre and one at each corner. Top up the potting compost and water well.

GOOD ADVICE
• You don't need to deadhead these begonias, but it's worth picking up fallen flowers as they can mark the leaves while they decompose.

• Why not plant a selection of 'Non Stop' begonias, including the gorgeous tangerine included here, giving each colour a container to itself.

• Be adventurous and include some varieties grown for their beautiful leaves. *Begonias rex*, for example, will enjoy a summer holiday in the garden, given shade and shelter.

• You can keep your begonias from year to year by saving the corms. When the leaves have been touched by frost, dig them up and dry them off in a shed or greenhouse. Once the leaves and stems have fallen off, plunge them in old, dry potting compost for the winter, keeping them cool but frost-free. Start them off into growth again in spring by potting them up.

Everlasting Pleasure

Although perhaps more associated with dried indoor arrangements than border or container displays, the hot colours of strawflowers can transform a bare patch into a fiery furnace of colour and 'Bright Bikinis' is the best dwarf strain I've grown. They mix well with other sun-loving daisies like zinnias, but I chose to pick up the dry, bristly texture of the petals by packing them into a wicker basket with their pots buried in hay and edged up with a collection of dried sunflower heads that were allowed to wither *in situ* on their thick stems. I was so pleased with the results that next year I plan to add other 'dried flowers' such as statice and love-lies-bleeding in separate baskets to build up the display.

YOU WILL NEED
a wicker basket, 40 cm (16 in) in diameter and at least 15 cm (6 in) deep · 24 dwarf strawflowers (*Helichrysum bracteatum* 'Bright Bikinis') · 12 dried sunflower heads (*Helianthus*)

PERIOD OF INTEREST
July to September

LOCATION
In an open sunny spot. If the basket is strong enough it can even be suspended outside a window.

FOR CONTINUITY
Grow some extra strawflowers to plant out in a nursery bed for cutting and drying and combine them with the sunflower heads to repeat the theme indoors over the winter.

1 Strawflowers can be raised from seed sown indoors in April and pricked out into a seed tray. In 4–6 weeks, transfer the young plants into 12.5 cm (5 in) pots. Sunflowers can be sown straight into the border in May.

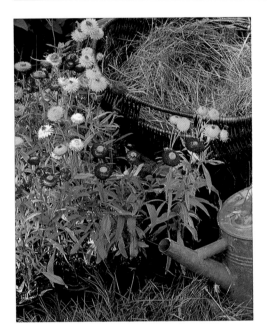

2 When the strawflowers are beginning to show colour, bury them – pot and all – in a mulch of hay within the wicker basket. Finish off the arrangement by inserting the dried sunflower heads.

GOOD ADVICE
● Snip off the strawflowers when they are fully expanded and are beginning to go brown in the centre to encourage more flowers to develop.
● For indoor decoration it is vital to pick strawflowers just as they are beginning to open.

1 *strawflowers*
2 *sunflowers*

Flower Festival

If spring comes early and you haven't planted many late spring-flowering bulbs like tulips, you may find a bit of a gap developing in your container display in May, yet it is too early to plant out the summer bedding – except in only the very mildest parts of the country. For times like this, varieties that will tolerate a few cold nights or even a touch of frost are a godsend, and osteospermums – those prolific South African daisies – are amongst the best. Pansies, too, are good for it is now that they peak. There's a good chance you will have pansies in full bloom, but if not there are still plenty on sale. With luck, you may even find the lovely, ginger-coloured flowers that I've used in this flower festival display, and which harmonise so well with the terracotta.

YOU WILL NEED
a shallow, terracotta bowl, 50 cm (20 in) in diameter · 3 contrasting osteospermums (O. 'Sunny Lady', O. 'Buttermilk' and O. 'Silver Sparkler') · 5 pansies (*Viola* x *wittrockiana*) in mixed colours
broken crocks

PERIOD OF INTEREST
May to September

LOCATION
In full sun. For greater impact, raise the bowl up higher on an upturned pot.

FOR CONTINUITY
By July the pansies will begin to get leggy so cut them back hard and plant them in a border. Replace with pot-grown coneflowers.

1 Select your osteospermums and pansies in May. There are usually plenty of variations to choose from. Water them thoroughly. Then fill the bowl to within 5–7.5 cm (2–3 in) of the rim with potting compost.

2 Put the three osteospermums in position, spaced around the bowl, then fill in around them with the pansies. Top up with potting compost. As a finishing touch, use some broken crocks to make an edging around the bowl. Water well to settle in the plants.

GOOD ADVICE
● Broken crocks placed around the edge of the bowl not only look good but stop the potting compost washing over the edge.
● Regular deadheading is essential to keep up the show.
● Overwinter the osteospermums in cool, frost-free conditions.

1 *Osteospermum 'Sunny Lady'*
2 *Osteospermum 'Buttermilk'*
3 *Osteospermum 'Silver Sparkler'*
4 *pansies*

In the Pink

Searching for a theme can often cause problems for the container gardener faced with a wide range of (empty) containers and an almost overwhelming choice of plants. So, in the same way as when I'm designing a garden, I look for a suitable starting point. In this case it was some silver-leaved senecios left over from the previous year. They were a bit unkempt but redeemable and would provide a perfect foil for a pastel scheme.

Pink seemed the obvious choice. It is the most popular, bedding plant colour, though it can clash with new, orangey red terracotta. Luckily my pot was well weathered with moss and chalk deposits, which would echo the grey and green in the planting. I then chose a tall plant, two bushy plants and three trailers to create a well-balanced display.

YOU WILL NEED
a well-weathered, terracotta pot, 45 cm (18 in) in diameter · 3 *Senecio cineraria* 'Cirrus' · 1 pink marguerite (*Argyranthemum* 'Vancouver') 2 *Pelargonium* 'Lovesong' · 3 *Verbena* 'Sissinghurst'

PERIOD OF INTEREST
June to September

LOCATION
In full sun, with plenty of space around the pot so the verbena can spread.

FOR CONTINUITY
Deadhead the pelargonium and marguerite every week. Cut off any flowering shoots on the senecio.

1 Assemble the plants, and water them thoroughly until they are all nicely moist in their containers.

2 If you are refurbishing a pot that already contains some plants, carefully dig around them with a trowel; try not to disturb their roots unduly. Then remove the top 15 cm (6 in) of potting compost.

3 Top up with fresh potting compost to within 7.5 cm (3 in) of the rim. Plant the marguerite towards the centre, flanked by the pelargoniums and then put the trailing verbenas around the outside. Water the pot well.

GOOD ADVICE
● You can speed up the ageing process on a new terracotta pot by painting on live yoghurt.
● Silver-leaved senecios can easily be raised from seed or bought as young plants.

1 *senecio*
2 *marguerite*
3 *pelargonium*
4 *verbena*

Trail Blazers

One of the most exciting plant introductions of recent years has been a new race of super-vigorous hybrid petunias that can put on up to 2 m (6½ ft) of growth in a single season. They now sell by the million as young, pot-grown plants or smaller plug plants and are all struck from cuttings taken from mother plants at the nursery. If you are not used to such rampant growth rates, these hybrid petunias can quickly get the better of you, so my advice is threefold.

Firstly, select a tall container so that the petunias can cascade over the edge. Secondly, pair up these petunias only with equally robust plants, and, thirdly, keep pinching them out, especially in the early stages of growth, so that you encourage a bushy cascade, not just a few overlong trails.

YOU WILL NEED
a reconstituted-stone urn, 35 cm (14 in) in diameter, sitting on a pedestal
polystyrene chunks · 2 *Petunia* 'Surfinia'
4 tapien verbenas (*V.* 'Tapien Pink' and *V.* 'Tapien Violet') · 2 *Helichrysum petiolare*

PERIOD OF INTEREST
June to September

LOCATION
In sun, raised up in a border and backed by planting or against a wall or hedge.

FOR CONTINUITY
Liquid feed every 7–10 days or add a slow-release feed, which works for a whole season, to the potting compost.

74

1 Pack out the bottom third of the urn with broken polystyrene and then fill up with potting compost to within 5–7.5 cm (2–3 in) of the rim. Assemble your plants and water well.

2 Move the pots around until an attractive display is achieved. Then plant the petunias in the middle, and space out the verbenas around them. Put the grey helichrysums on opposite sides.

3 Finally pinch out the petunias to build up a strong framework of shoots, and water the compost thoroughly to settle in the plants.

GOOD ADVICE
● Pinch out the grey helichrysums a few times to encourage them to bush out.
● If you are prepared to wait a bit longer for the urn display to fill out, reduce the plant quantities by half.

1 *petunias*
2 *verbenas*
3 *helichrysums*

Ice and Lemon

All-white colour schemes (if white is a colour) have never really gone out of fashion, but on dull, overcast days they can look a little dreary. One solution is to add a splash of yellow, which gives white leaves and flowers a really refreshing zing. In early summer there is plenty of yellow to pick from, though the two in my ice-and-lemon cube are amongst the most outstanding and richly coloured; they will also flower continuously till the frosts arrive.

My favourite container creations are ones that feature foliage and flowers, and ornamental cabbage and kale are worthy contenders. As the evenings get cooler, the leaf colours intensify and peak in late summer and autumn. As well as white, there are pink and purple selections to fire your imagination.

YOU WILL NEED
a terracotta pot, 40 cm (16 in) square
1 ornamental cabbage Northern Lights
Series · 2 *Calceolaria* 'Sunshine'
1 strawflower (*Helichrysum bracteatum*
'Dargan Hill Monarch') · 2 white petunias
2 white New Guinea busy lizzies
(*Impatiens*, New Guinea Hybrids)

PERIOD OF INTEREST
June to September

LOCATION
In sun or semi-shade. A pair would look
good flanking a door.

FOR CONTINUITY
Pinch out fading petunia flowers before
they run to seed and snip off the oldest
strawflowers as they discolour.

1 After assembling your plants, dunk any that are dry in a bowl of water for a couple of hours before planting. (Ornamental cabbages, calceolarias and strawflowers can be bought as younger plants if you prefer.)

2 Half fill your container with potting compost. Then, with the plants still in their pots, make a pleasing arrangement, keeping the taller plants – cabbage, calceolarias and petunias – to the rear of the planter.

3 Working from the centre to the edge of the planter, carefully knock each plant out of its pot – protecting its roots and the rest of the plants from its compost – and plant it up. Top up the potting compost and water well.

GOOD ADVICE
● To add an 'antique' finish to a new terracotta pot, paint on a thin solution of lime and water, as I've done here. Always wear protective gloves and goggles.

1 *ornamental cabbage*
2 *calceolarias*
3 *strawflowers*
4 *petunias*
5 *busy lizzies*

Monkey Business

Monkey musk, or mimulus, is amongst the most extrovert of garden flowers, and it reveals an almost-human quality in the way its blooms peer around to face each other. Its particularly vivid flowers are often speckled and spotted within, as in a deep-throated orchid. Monkey musks love moisture and the more they get the merrier they will be. This fact more than compensates for their somewhat restricted flowering period compared to, say, the trailing lobelia that I have partnered them with here. If you are brave enough, let the lobelia wander through the bright yellow leaves of the deadnettle and yellow-leaved creeping Jenny, and every tiny flower will be thrown into sharp focus. Fortune favours the brave as they say.

YOU WILL NEED
a terracotta pot, 40 cm (16 in) in diameter
2 plain monkey musk (*Mimulus* 'Malibu Orange') · 1 spotted monkey musk (*Mimulus*) · 2 yellow-leaved deadnettles (*Lamium maculatum* 'Aureum') · 3 yellow-leaved creeping Jenny (*Lysimachia nummularia* 'Aurea') · 2 trailing lobelia (*L. richardsonii*)

PERIOD OF INTEREST
June and July

LOCATION
In half sun or full shade. Hostas would look good alongside.

FOR CONTINUITY
Replace the monkey musk with pot-grown dwarf coneflowers or chrysanthemums.

1 Sow the monkey musk in March in a heated greenhouse or on an indoor windowsill. Or, buy plants as they are coming into bloom along with the lobelia and foliage plants. Almost fill the pot with potting compost.

2 Interplant the deadnettle and creeping Jenny along the front edge, then add the two lobelias behind. Finally plant the monkey musks at the back. Top up with more potting compost if necessary, and then give the plants a good soaking to settle them.

GOOD ADVICE
● Overwinter the perennial *Lobelia richardsonii* in frost-free conditions and bring it into active growth again the following spring.

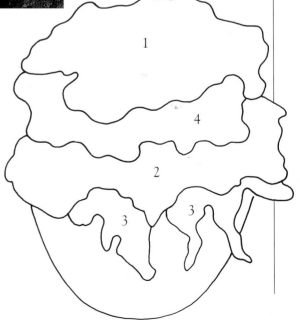

1 *monkey musk*
2 *deadnettle*
3 *creeping Jenny*
4 *lobelia*

Salad Days

Digging up parsnips and carrots has a certain excitement to it, but it can't match the pleasurable anticipation when the first, home-grown salad crops are imminent. Even if tomatoes were inedible (they were at first thought to be poisonous), the dwarf bush and trailing varieties would still be worth growing just for their ornamental value. 'Red Robin' – an ultra dwarf tomato and less domineering than the more familiar 'Tumbler' – makes an excellent focal point in an edible container.

For a longer-lasting show, select varieties you can pick over like 'Lollo Rossa' lettuce rather than those that are cut whole, leaving a gap. You can also mix in some of the more refined culinary herbs like basil and parsley, while tagetes will inject some extra colour and (some believe) deter sap-sucking insects.

YOU WILL NEED
a plastic pot, 40 cm (16 in) square
2 dwarf bush tomatoes 'Red Robin'
3 pale orange tagetes (*T.* 'Tangerine Gem')
2 parsley (*Petroselinum*) · 9 basil
(*Ocimum basilicum*) · 3 dwarf lettuce
'Little Leprechaun'

PERIOD OF INTEREST
June to September

LOCATION
In sun and shelter. Near the kitchen door would be convenient.

FOR CONTINUITY
Sow two or three batches of lettuce in small pots to replace harvested plants.

---

1 Select your favourite salad vegetables and herbs. They can be grown from seed or bought as young plants. Sow the basil seed indoors in May; basil is very sensitive to cold so don't sow it any earlier than this.

2 Almost fill the pot with potting compost. Plant the tomatoes towards the back surrounded by the tagetes and flanked by the parsley. Add a row of basil, then dwarf lettuce to edge up.

3 Top up the compost to a maximum of 2.5cm (1in) below the rim, so the compost does not get washed over the edge while watering. Place the pot under glass if you are keen for quick results.

GOOD ADVICE
● Pick over the herbs regularly to keep them bushy and compact.
● Feed all the plants every week with a tomato fertiliser.

1 *tomatoes*
2 *tagetes*
3 *parsley*
4 *basil*
5 *lettuce*

Strawberry Surprise

Strawberries – as you doubtless know – come in all shapes and sizes, from the tiny delectable alpine forms to juicy monsters as big as a child's fist, but have you seen pink-flowered and variegated plants? They really are attractive, especially at flowering time, though I should warn you not to expect great bowlfuls of fruit. I counted eight strawberries on these three plants: the birds ate three and the children had the rest so I can't vouch for the flavour! Anyway, this display provides a real conversation piece that improves with age as the runners descend over the sides like mountaineers on ropes. Because the fruits are raised off the ground, they are more likely to escape attack by slugs and won't get splashed with mud. In fact, I've convinced myself that next year my strawberry surprise could well form the centrepiece of a mobile strawberry patch.

YOU WILL NEED
a clay pan, 30 cm (12 in) in diameter and
15 cm (6 in) deep · 2 pink strawberries
'Ruby Surprise' · 1 variegated strawberry
fine stone chippings

PERIOD OF INTEREST
May to September

LOCATION
In sun, sheltered from cold winds.

FOR CONTINUITY
Add trailing lobelia between the
strawberry plants to give colour between
the flushes of strawberry flowers.

1 Assemble your strawberry plants in April or May. These specimen-sized plants will give almost instant maturity, but smaller ones will do. Put a layer of potting compost in the bottom of your pan.

2 Plant the pink and variegated plants. Fill in the gaps with more potting compost, ensuring you don't bury the centre of your plants with compost or they may rot. Use a sprayer to clean any compost off the leaves.

3 Finally add the finishing touch – a dressing of fine stone chippings. This prevents the potting compost from washing away and provides good surface drainage. Give the plants a good soaking to settle them in.

GOOD ADVICE
• As runners form, stand the pan up on another pot so they hang down freely, or peg them into small pots alongside and let them root.
• Watch out for infestations of greenfly. Squeeze them between your fingers to control them.
• As an alternative to 'Ruby Surprise', try 'Pink Panda'.

1 *pink strawberries*
2 *variegated strawberry*

82

Daisy Pot

The diversity amongst the daisy family is truly amazing and even if you had a hundred varieties you'd never get bored or want for colour, at least in summer and autumn when they're out in force. They're real charmers and well worth a pot to themselves.

You can plant up a daisy pot using easily available, off-the-shelf summer bedding plants, but I grew most of these from seed. It's more time consuming, but great fun and worth the effort, because you can be sure that no one else will have anything like it and you can tease your garden visitors with some of the more unusual varieties. By sowing in April and planting up in mid- to late June, your daisy pot will peak in late summer and autumn, when flower colour is becoming more scarce.

YOU WILL NEED
a terracotta pot, 55 cm (22 in) in diameter
9 coneflowers (*Rudbeckia hirta* 'Rustic Dwarfs') · 7 dwarf strawflowers
(*Helichrysum bracteatum* 'Dwarf Hot Bikini')
7 *Oncosiphon grandiflorum*,
syn. *Matricaria grandiflora* 'Gold Pompoms'
2 dwarf tickseeds (*Coreopsis tinctoria*)

PERIOD OF INTEREST
July to October

LOCATION
In full sun, surrounded by foliage as a foil to the bright colours.

FOR CONTINUITY
Aim for one big explosion of colour, then after the first frost concentrate on winter-interest plants.

1 Raise the annuals – coneflowers, strawflowers and oncosiphons – from seed in April. After 3–4 weeks, prick them out into seed trays, 24 plants per tray. In mid- to late June, almost fill the pot with potting compost.

2 Plant the tickseeds in the centre, then fill in around the back with coneflowers, carefully separated out from the seed tray. Put the strawflowers and oncosiphon around the edges and at the front. Water in well.

3 The plants will soon pick up as they make fresh root growth and become established. Then sit back and wait for the show!

GOOD ADVICE
● If you raise a seed tray of each of the annuals, you will have enough for fresh floral arrangements (coneflowers) and for drying (strawflowers and oncosiphons)
● Yellow *Coreopsis verticillata* would be just as good as red *C. tinctoria*.

1 *coneflowers*
2 *strawflowers*
3 *oncosiphons*
4 *tickseeds*

Autumn in the Air

You've got to admire michaelmas daisies. They respond to reduced daylight and falling temperatures and are genuine autumn-flowering plants. It is often November before they falter. Although not often associated with pots, the keen container gardener will want to make the most of these little gems. Another indispensable plant for summer and autumn is houttuynia. The heart-shaped, pink-and-yellow-splashed leaves make a terrific edging to a pot or trough and knits together in only a few weeks. *Fuchsia* 'Versicolor' sits well alongside with its arching shoots clothed with soft grey-green, variegated leaves and slim, pendant, purple, red-skirted blooms. Beneath this I slipped in a trailing knotweed whose leaves were taking on vivid autumn tints.

YOU WILL NEED
a plastic trough, 35 cm (14 in) x 55cm (22 in) · 2 dwarf michaelmas daisies (*Aster novi-belgii* 'Lady in Blue') · 2 *Houttuynia* 'Joseph's Coat' · 1 *Fuchsia* 'Versicolor' 1 knotweed (*Polygonum affine* 'Darjeeling Red')

PERIOD OF INTEREST
September to November

LOCATION
In sun or shade against a wall where a Virginia creeper or ornamental grape vine is colouring up.

FOR CONTINUITY
Add autumn crocus or colchicum bulbs along the front to strengthen the display.

Move the plant containers around until you have a satisfactory display. Then half fill the trough with compost. Insert the daisies at the back filling in with the other plants. Top up with compost and water. This arrangement looks better than a symmetrical one with the fuchsia in the centre.

GOOD ADVICE
● Pull out the trough plants in November and plant them in a border. If you wish to feature them again in pots, dig them up the following May.
● To avoid mildew, choose more resistant varieties like *Aster thomsonii* 'Nanus' and *A. amellus* 'Violet Queen' or spray every two weeks in summer with a fungicide.
● Don't forget to drill drainage holes in new plastic containers. Use a battery-powered drill for this.
● Why not use this trough as the centrepiece of an autumn display on a theme of gathering in the harvest. Set ornamental gourds, striped marrows and pumpkins around the base.

1 *michaelmas daisies*
2 *houttuynia*
3 *fuchsia*
4 *knotweed*

Two-tier Miniatures

Tiny treasures such as these violets and hardy cyclamen can easily be intimidated by outsized containers and overbearing neighbours, so I set out to make a mini landscape where they could be shown off in all their glory. It consisted of two clay pans, one perched on top of the other, with the lower one edged with a dwarf hedge of golden euonymus. When complete it looked as inviting as a wedding cake. To fill the gap between the euonymus stems and the pan side, and to give a decorated edge like piped icing, I slipped in houseleeks. These and the euonymus make a permanent frame that looks good throughout the year. Within the circle, plants can be swapped, so there is always something of interest.

1 Loosen the rootball of the euonymus, separating it into individual plants that can be spread evenly around the pan edge.

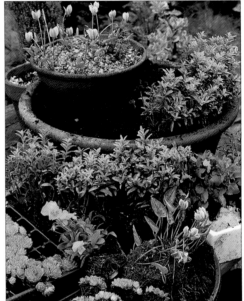

2 Assemble the plants. Fill the top pan with potting compost and plant it full of cyclamen and sagina. Then half fill the lower pan with compost. Plant the euonymus hedge towards the edge. Fill in with the violets, and finally insert the houseleek edging. Add more compost and water both pans well to settle the plants in.

YOU WILL NEED
2 terracotta pans 25 cm (10 in) in diameter and 46 cm (18 in) in diameter · 3 bedding violas · 3 *Cyclamen hederifolium* (syn. *C. neapolitanum*) · 1 *Sagina glabra* 'Aurea' · 4 pots of mini, gold-variegated euonymus (*E. japonicus* 'Microphyllus Aureovariegatus') · 18 houseleeks (*Sempervivum*)

PERIOD OF INTEREST
September to November

LOCATION
In sun or semi-shade, preferably raised up.

FOR CONTINUITY
Underplant the cyclamen with crocus and *Iris reticulata* bulbs to give colour in winter and spring.

GOOD ADVICE
• The best way to purchase hardy cyclamen is actively growing in pots. From dry corms they are slow and rarely as successful.
• Buy the variegated euonymus as rooted cuttings – several to a pot.
• Clip the mini euonymus hedge with scissors two or three times a year to keep it compact.

1 *violets*
2 *cyclamen*
3 *sagina*
4 *euonymus*
5 *houseleeks*

Winter Warmer

Some plants look as though they have no business being outdoors in the dead of winter, let alone to be flowering their heads off. Tiny *Cyclamen coum* looks so delicate that it comes as quite a surprise to learn that it is in fact very tough. It also self-seeds very readily.

The best way to buy cyclamen is as young plants already in leaf and bud – not as dry corms that are reluctant to sprout and prone to rotting. I bought four *Cyclamen coum* from a local nursery in February, selecting them as much for their attractive leaf patterns as for their flowers.

It's important not to overpower such tiny treasures by putting them in enormous containers or with outsized companions, so here I selected some cheerful, dwarf, variegated evergreens.

YOU WILL NEED

a shallow, terracotta pan, 30 cm (12 in) x 20 cm (8 in) · 1 dwarf, variegated sedge (*Carex oshimensis* 'Evergold') · 1 variegated osmanthus (*O. heterophyllus* 'Goshiki') 1 dwarf, variegated euonymus 4 *Cyclamen coum*

PERIOD OF INTEREST
January to March

LOCATION
In sun or semi-shade, raised up where the pan can be seen from house, or on a balcony or in an unheated porch.

FOR CONTINUITY
Replace the cyclamen with pot-grown *Tulipa tarda* in early spring.

Choose a suitable pan of similar proportions to those shown here. There are several types on the market including glazed, bonsai pans. Fill it with potting compost to within 5–7.5 cm (2–3 in) of the rim. Plant the sedge so it will spill over the front. Position the osmanthus and euonymus at the back, and then fill in the gaps with the cyclamen still in their original pots. Top up the compost and water well.

GOOD ADVICE
• Stand the pan on four terracotta pot feet to improve its appearance. Such feet also prevent worms entering from below and blocking the drainage holes.
• To increase surface drainage, topdress the pan with small stone chippings.
• After flowering, you could remove the evergreens, plant the cyclamen properly and let them colonise the pan.

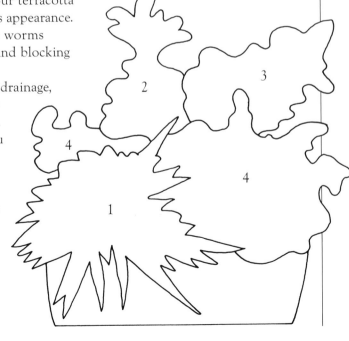

1 *sedge*
2 *osmanthus*
3 *euonymus*
4 *cyclamen*

Roses Revealed

Perhaps the most outstanding, winter-flowering herbaceous plant is the Lenten rose, which is far more likely to succeed in a container than the temperamental Christmas rose, *Helleborus niger*. The Lenten rose is hardy, flowers for weeks, and comes in a ravishing range of flower colours, some speckled or spotted. Its only drawback is that its nodding flowers tend to hang down, hiding their faces and the prominent stamens. To avoid this problem, plant it in a tall container like this Gothic font so you can greet it at eye level. To give additional support, station evergreens in front of your Lenten rose. I restricted this container to three colours – yellow, purple and pink – but nothing could outshine the ravishing Lenten rose.

YOU WILL NEED
a tall planter or urn, 38 cm (15 in) in diameter or sit a terracotta pot on another upturned pot or brick pier · ericaceous potting compost · 1–2 Lenten roses (*Helleborus orientalis*) · 1 female pernettya (in fruit) · 1 *Acorus gramineus* 'Ogon' 1 *Euonymus japonicus* 'Aureus' 12–16 crocus bulbs (*C. luteus* 'Dutch Yellow', syn. C. 'Yellow Giant') · moss

PERIOD OF INTEREST
January to early April

LOCATION
In sun or shade under a deciduous tree.

FOR CONTINUITY
Replace the yellow crocuses as they fade with primroses (*Primula vulgaris*) to maintain the yellow theme.

1 Assemble all the plants and, with the Lenten rose at the back, move the other containers around until the arrangement is visually satisfying.

2 Half fill the urn with ericaceous potting compost. Cut away all the old leaves from the Lenten rose before planting it at the back of the urn. (Fresh new leaves will quickly follow.) Then plant the pernettya, acorus, euonymus and crocus. Top up the compost and add a dressing of moss. Finally water everything well.

GOOD ADVICE
● The female pernettya will need a male plant nearby to produce berries for the following season. It also needs lime-free soil.

1 *Lenten rose*
2 *pernettya*
3 *acorus*
4 *euonymus*
5 *crocus*

92

Air Freshener

You might be surprised to learn how many winter-flowering shrubs, such as witch hazel, winter honeysuckles, viburnum and sarcococca (seen here), have a spicy, penetrating perfume, yet none has flowers bigger than a 10 pence piece. Conveniently, gardeners can harness these tantalising scents by planning a winter air freshener – a container packed with all the best that's on offer to flower all together in one glorious pot-pourri, or one containing flowers that bloom consecutively so that there is a different scent on offer every week or two. The basic framework of evergreens, with scented leaves, flowers or both, can be supplemented by a selection of dwarf scented bulbs, such as iris and hyacinths, and wallflowers.

YOU WILL NEED
a galvanised dolly tub, 40 cm (16 in) in diameter · polystyrene chunks or plastic bags · 1 *Choisya* 'Sundance'
1 sarcococca · 3 wallflowers (*Erysimum*)
1 trailing yellow conifer (*Chamaecyparis pisifera* 'Filifera Aureomarginata')
5 mixed pots of dwarf iris (*Iris reticulata*)

PERIOD OF INTEREST
February to early May

LOCATION
In a warm, sheltered spot, near a door or window, preferably raised up for effortless sniffing!

FOR CONTINUITY
Replace the iris with hyacinths or dwarf scented daffodils like *Narcissus* 'Baby Moon' to flower with the wallflowers.

1 For temporary displays, deep containers like half beer barrels or this dolly tub can be packed out to half their depth with polystyrene chunks or screwed up plastic bags to save on potting compost.

2 Gather the scented selection of plants together and check they are in good condition. Remove any dead or damaged shoots. Then add a good layer of potting compost to the tub, firming it gently to remove any air holes.

3 Plant the choisya, sarcococca, wallflowers, and trailing conifer, firming the soil around their roots. Carefully knock out the iris and slip them in amongst the evergreens. Top up the compost and water well.

GOOD ADVICE
● Keep an eye out for wilting leaves. Even in winter, frosts and cold winds can sap moisture from leaves and roots.
● Why not leave the yellow evergreen in place as the basis for a summer display.

1 *choisya*
2 *sarcococca*
3 *wallflowers*
4 *conifer*
5 *iris*

The Festive Touch

That Christmas tree so eagerly anticipated, painstakingly selected and given pride of place in the lounge becomes a waste disposal problem after Twelfth Night. My 'Christmas tree' starts off as a snug potful of coloured evergreens planted up in November, dressed with home-grown garden decorations for the festive season and afterwards acts as the perfect host to show off small potfuls of spring bulbs, polyanthus and pansies. Well, alright, it may not actually be in the lounge, but most homes have got a window or two where a special seasonal container, like this, can be laid on near enough to the house to allow armchair viewing.

YOU WILL NEED
a decorated terracotta pot, 48 cm (19 in) in diameter · 1 juniper (*Juniperus* 'Grey Owl') · 1 specimen-sized *Osmanthus heterophyllus* 'Goshiki' or variegated elaeagnus 1 *Chamaecyparis pisifera* 'Squarrosa Lombarts' · 1 tree heather (*Erica arborea* 'Albert's Gold') · 1 *Skimmia* 'Rubella'
OPTIONAL
honesty (*Lunaria*) · gladwin (*Iris foetidissima*) · old man's beard (*Clematis*)

PERIOD OF INTEREST
October to April

LOCATION
In sun or shade, on a balcony or porch or in a cool conservatory.

FOR CONTINUITY
Use dazzling, dwarf, red tulips like 'Red Riding Hood' to flower alongside the skimmia in spring.

96

1 The project got off to a flying start. A 'Grey Owl' juniper from a previous display was left *in situ* at the front of the pot, while as much potting compost as possible was changed without disturbing the juniper's rootball.

2 Position the taller evergreen at the back and bank down the heights saving the most prominent spot for the red-budded skimmia. Top up with more potting compost and water thoroughly to settle the plants in.

3 For a change of mood, add cut stems of dried honesty, gladwin and old man's beard. After dark you can bring the display alive with an uplighter skimming the outline of the pot.

GOOD ADVICE
● Avoid the gladwin if children might be tempted to eat its poisonous berries.
● A floodlight or outdoor fairy lights are also good accent lights.

1 *juniper*
2 *osmanthus*
3 *chamaecyparis*
4 *tree heather*
5 *skimmia*

LOOKING AFTER YOUR CONTAINERS

Caring for plants in pots is like raising children. They are entirely dependent on you, but if you look after them they will constantly reward you, and if you have enough of them there will be something new to delight and captivate you every few days.

My number one tip is to get to know your plants. They will tell you when they're unhappy and the earlier you pick up their distress signals the better. It's natural to reach for the watering can as soon as you see stems and leaves wilting, but this is not always because they're dry. A waterlogged plant will wilt, as will one whose roots are being devoured by vine weevil grubs. Shiny trails of slime on leaves are a sure sign that slugs and snails have been at work munching your precious plants overnight.

Once you're into a regular routine of watering and feeding and really watching your container display, the rapport will soon build up. Professional growers never let their plants suffer stress through lack of water or nutrients. Their plants grow evenly without any stunting or yellowing of leaves that can result from crisis management.

The one job I really hate is using chemicals to control pests and diseases. I'd like to think that natural predators would wipe out those greenfly, but by the time the ladybirds are out in force, the plant is often half ruined; careful observation and early action are therefore vital.

A Simple Guide to Perfect Containers

Essential equipment

- Fold-up sheet for protecting paving as you plant up your containers.
- Hand fork for loosening compacted potting compost.
- Trowel for planting and grubbing out spent plants.
- Secateurs or scissors for pruning and deadheading plants.
- Watering can, preferably a long-necked, well-balanced one with a fine rose for watering seedlings.
- Trigger pump sprayer for cleaning leaves and a separate one for spraying pesticides. Write 'poison' on the one for chemicals and keep it out of reach of children.
- Gloves – some plants can irritate the skin.

Potting composts

There are two main types of potting compost: loam- or soil-based mixes such as John Innes; and soil-less potting composts, which traditionally are of peat, blended with sharp sand and a slow-release fertiliser. As environmental concerns for peat bogs deepen, coconut fibre (coir) and shredded bark alternatives are being introduced, which can give excellent results. Soil-based mixes are better for long-term planting and larger specimens. Soil-less composts are often suitable for sowing and potting; they are also cleaner and easier to handle than soil-based ones but do lose water and nutrients more rapidly. Sand, gravel, mica or vermiculite can be added to improve drainage.

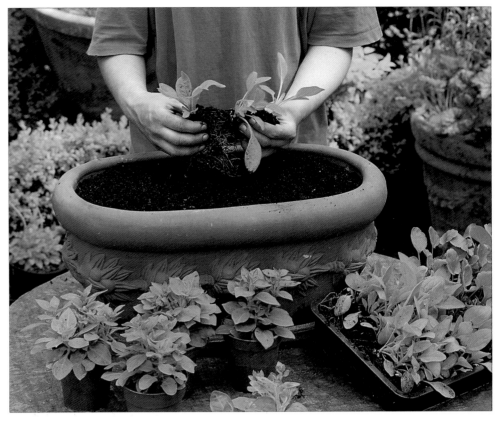

Advance planning

- Soak new terracotta pots overnight by immersing them in a tank of water to prevent them drawing moisture out of the potting compost.
- Drill drainage holes in the base of new plastic containers, using a battery-powered drill. Plastic containers often have half-pierced holes marked out, and these just require a thin layer of plastic removing. Do not press too hard on the drill, or the plastic base may crack.
- Treat wicker baskets with two or three coats of clear preservative or two or three coats of waterproofing, yacht varnish.
- Set heavy stone pots and troughs into their final positions before you add any potting compost or plants. After planting, they may be too heavy to move.

Separate young plants by gently teasing apart the roots like this, the aim being to retain an equal amount of roots on each young plant.

- Set flat-bottomed containers on bricks or proprietary pot feet to raise them off the ground. This improves their appearance and prevents worms from entering and blocking the drainage holes.
- Use an ericaceous (lime-free) potting compost for acid-loving plants such as camellias and summer-flowering heathers.
- Before planting summer containers, mix water-retaining gel with the potting compost at the recommended rate to increase moisture-holding capacity.
- Wet potting compost that is dry and powdery until it is just damp

enough to stay in a ball when squeezed in the hand.

• For containers that will house the same plants for several years, fill up the bottom quarter of the container with drainage material such as crocks or gravel.

Planting up

• Start with clean containers, seed trays and pots; scrubbing them thoroughly in detergent will reduce infection from pests and diseases.

• Assemble your plants, working to a special theme, colour scheme or just a dazzling splash of colour! It is often a good idea to mix together plants of contrasting habit in the same pot so it fills out from top to bottom. Consider also whether you want an 'instant' display that looks good from day one, or one that will improve or peak with age.

With pot-grown bedding, make a hole for the plant in the compost. Carefully tuck in the plant and firm the compost using light pressure.

• Decide on which direction the pot will be seen from so there will be a definite front and back. There's no point in wasting trailers if no light gets to the back of the pot. Alternatively, as a centrepiece on a patio, it may be viewed from all sides so ensure interest all round.

• Avoid vigorous trailers in a container with attractive decoration on the sides, or it will be hidden.

• Make sure all your recipe plants are well watered before putting them into their display pot.

• Save on the amount of potting compost needed in large containers by filling the base with polystyrene chips from packaging material or old plastic bags scrunched up so as not to impede drainage.

• Lightly tap the rim of the pot on the workbench to loosen the rootball before taking out the plant and supporting it between your fingers.

• Position the plant with the deepest rootball in the pot first, having beforehand added sufficient potting compost in the base so that its level

If the rootballs of your pot-grown bedding plants are wrapped in tightly bound roots, gently tease out the roots to encourage new ones to form in the fresh potting compost.

is 2.5–5 cm (1–2 in) below the rim. Fill in with more compost, then put in the other plants.

• Keep the soil off flowers and leaves as it is particularly hard to dislodge from hairy plants such as tobacco plants and petunias.

• Plants at the edge of a container display can be angled slightly to encourage them to drape over the sides of the container.

• After planting, carefully firm the potting compost around the plant roots. Then gently knock the container a few times on the ground to settle the compost.

• Add slow-release, push-in fertiliser pellets or sticks to the compost.

• Level the potting compost to within 2.5–5 cm (1–2 in) of the container rim so that the compost does not wash over the edge while the plants are watered.

• Sit back and enjoy your container once you've watered everything well!

Growing Tips

Selecting a site

- Some container plants do well in shade, others demand sun, but many will grow well in both sun and shade.
- Avoid planting under trees such as limes and sycamores, because such trees attract aphids, which drop sugary sap on to the plants below. These then get covered in black sooty mould.
- You can override your garden's natural soil conditions by growing plants in containers. You can, for example, enjoy acid-loving plants such as rhododendrons in a garden with limy soil by growing them in a pot filled with ericaceous potting compost, which is acidic. Alpines that demand good drainage can even be cultivated in gardens with waterlogged clay by isolating them in a trough and using a free-draining potting compost.
- Place tender blooms such as camellias near the house walls, where they will be more protected – but avoid east-facing aspects.
- In exposed sites, choose compact plants. Top-heavy pots will be blown over. Also, use a soil-based potting compost, which is heavier than a soil-less one, and add pebbles or broken bricks in the base of the container for extra stability.
- In coastal regions, salt spray may scorch leaves so select salt-tolerant plants such as hydrangeas and fuchsias in such areas.

Good husbandry

- Plants now come in a range of cells, trays, packs and pot sizes. Those that are bought through mail-order firms need potting up as soon as possible on arrival.
- Buy fresh, healthy plants free from water stress, pests and disease. Roots should not be restricted or protruding from the base of the container, and the overall shape should be bushy and well balanced.
- Try growing your own plants from seed, selecting those to suit your site, lifestyle and colour scheme. Carefully follow the instructions on the seed packet, and sow in seed

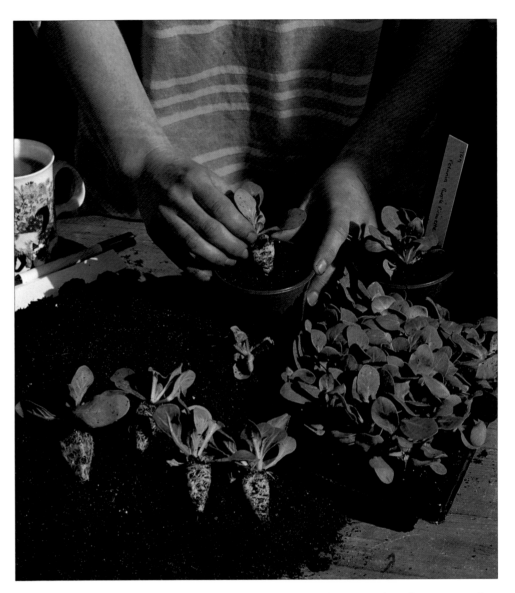

Bedding plants purchased as young plug or cell plants, potted up and grown on will cost less than half the price of more mature specimens.

trays or individual pots depending on the plant's size.
- Water seedlings from above, with a fine rose, or from below to limit disturbance.
- Once their leaves are large enough to handle, prick out the seedlings into seed trays to give them more

space in which to develop.

• Young plants can be transferred directly from seed trays to your display pots or grown on in individual pots to produce larger, more bushy specimens that will often be coming into flower and so give instant impact.

• Old, used potting compost may harbour pests and diseases and be low on nutrients, so always use fresh compost each time you plant – or at least replace the top half with new.

• Trim off any broken shoots, dead flower heads and seed pods and pinch back long, leggy shoots to encourage plants to bush out.

• Gradually harden off tender plants such as summer bedding and young

Below Take advantage of the flush of new growth in early summer to take cuttings and increase your stock of plants such as this yellow-leaved deadnettle.

Above Good-sized crowns of hostas like this can be sliced up into two or three separate pieces and grown on or planted straight into a display pot.

plants to outside temperatures. Always bring them inside at night if frost is forecast.

• Planting tender plants outside is usually not recommended until the first week in June.

• Prune any dead, damaged or diseased parts on a plant to maintain the health of topiary, trained specimens, climbers and shrubs.

• Label herbaceous plants before they die back in autumn, to avoid accidental loss.

• In spring or autumn, repot perennials and replace the top layer of potting compost around established trees and shrubs to give them a boost.

• Pay particular attention to drainage in winter time, when containers can become waterlogged. Bulbs for example are prone to rotting.

Care and Maintenance

Watering

• Water containers using a can with a fine rose or a hose nozzle that gives a gentle sprinkling of water, not a powerful jet.

• Water in the morning or evening to reduce evaporation and avoid splashing water on to foliage in bright sunshine, or it may scorch.

• Watering cannot be done to a pre-set timetable. How often water is needed depends on the planting, the type of container and its siting.

• Check each container daily in dry, sunny and windy conditions. Feel the compost with your fingers or lift the pot if you can. Look for early signs of wilting.

• Fill a dry container to the rim with water. Let it drain then repeat two or three times, or you'll wet only the surface even though water may appear through the bottom.

• Immerse a really dry plant in a bucket or bath of water overnight. It may be the only way to get water back into the rootball.

• Do not try to water any plants if frozen in their pots.

Feeding

• Feeding will keep your containers in tip-top condition, replacing nutrients used up by the plants or washed out through watering.

• Follow the manufacturer's

Regular deadheading will prevent the formation of seed, which would slow down or stop the production of fresh flower buds.

instructions and don't overdose.

• Solid or dry fertilisers can be mixed into the potting compost prior to planting, pushed into the surface, or applied as topdressings depending on their type. Some last for a whole season.

• Liquid feeds are concentrates, powders or granules sprayed through a special hose attachment or mixed up with water in a can. Apply every week or fortnightly.

• Foliar feeds act very quickly and correct trace element or mineral deficiencies.

• High-nitrogen feeds are good for foliage and potash ones are excellent for flowering, but a balanced fertiliser is best for mixed planting.

Maintenance tips

• Group your containers together to reduce maintenance time and give mutual protection from the weather.

• Regular pinching back of shoots will help plants such as fuchsias, pelargoniums, vigorous petunias and dwarf chrysanthemums (dendranthema) to bush out.

• Deadheading is essential for plants

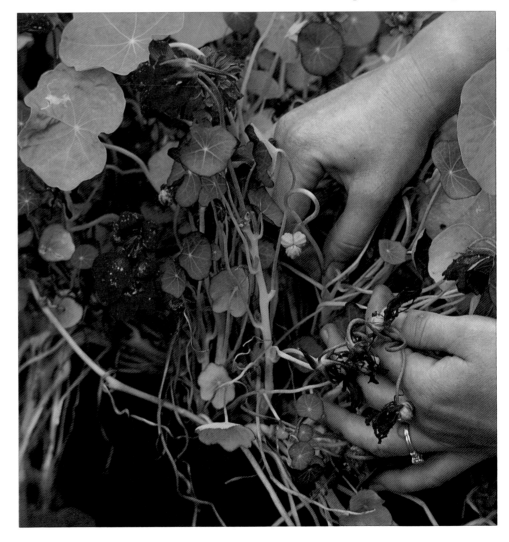

such as nasturtiums, pansies, dahlias, cosmos and marigolds to maintain appearances and keep the blooms coming over a long period.

• Various hose attachments are available to aid feeding and watering as well as high- or low-level, automatic irrigation systems.

• Move plants to sheltered, shaded areas if you're going away on holiday and, if no one else can water, stand them on capillary matting kept damp from a reservoir bucket of water. Some plants such as monkey musk can be stood in trays of water.

• Use a wheelbarrow, sack truck or trolley to move heavy or awkward containers or try rolling them along. Do not strain your back.

• Containers such as imported terracotta that are not frost proof should be emptied and moved

Below Settle in a newly planted pot by watering with the fine rose attachment on a can. If roots have been disturbed, stand the pot out of bright sun for a few days.

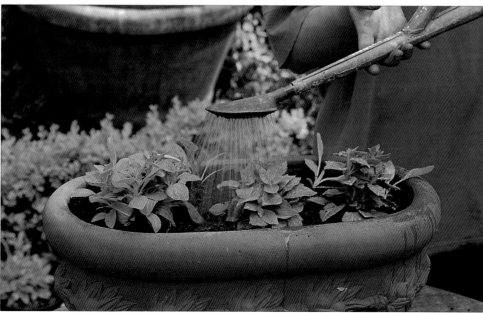

Above Protect the tender, young, red shoots of pieris with fleece at night if late frosts are forecast. Japanese maples will also appreciate this treatment.

somewhere dry and frost free for the winter to prevent splintering or cracking. Alternatively insulate them well with straw, polystyrene, bubble wrap or sacking. This also protects a plant's rootball from freezing solid.

• Move tender plants indoors before the frosts begin in the autumn or root cuttings so you will have new plants for the following summer.

• Knock off heavy snowfall from evergreens such as conifers, or their shape may be ruined.

Pests and diseases

To reduce significantly the incidence of pests and diseases, the golden rule
is to keep your plants healthy through regular care and maintenance.
Early detection can mean you merely need to squash pests in your fingers
or pick off infected leaves. If you do resort to chemicals, be sure to select
the appropriate one and follow the manufacturer's instructions. Plant-
based extracts can provide some of the safest substances.

PESTS/DISEASE	SYMPTOMS	TREATMENTS
Aphids: blackfly, greenfly, whitefly	Ragged petals, distorted buds, stunted growth, sticky honeydew deposits, sooty moulds or fungal infections or deposits. Spread of viral disease during feeding.	Squash small infestations by hand, wash with soapy water or spray with an appropriate insecticide. Do not overfeed with nitrogen, because aphids prefer the soft new growth that it promotes.
Ants	Disturbed soil around roots; foraging on aphids and transferring them to fresh sites.	Not a serious problem; best left alone.
Slugs and snails	Holes in leaves, particularly hostas, bulbs, rhizomes, tubers and damaged shoots.	Go out at night or in wet weather and pick snails off; keep areas tidy to restrict daytime hiding places; or place inverted pots as traps, emptying each morning. For slugs, use pellets or shallow sunken traps with sweet, enticing solutions, which drown visitors. Raise containers off the ground and mulch with grit to slow down their movement.
Leaf miners	White or brown tunnels in leaves created by the larvae of moths or flies. Marigolds and chrysanthemums are particularly prone.	Pick off and destroy affected leaves.
Red spider mites	Discolouring or speckling on leaves, with fine, silky webbing; mites on the underside. More prevalent in hot, dry conditions.	Pick off affected leaves and spray with an appropriate insecticide.
Vine weevils	Adult beetles make notches in leaves while the wrinkled, white larvae with darker heads curl up in compost. Roots, rhizomes and corms are destroyed; plants become stunted or die; compost loosens and crumbles.	Tidy up to restrict hiding places of adults during the day, collect at night. Inspect pots in spring and late summer. Squash grubs or apply nematode, biological control.

Left Search for snails hiding under leaves. Slugs prefer to creep into the soil or stay under a pot in the day.

Right As soon as tulips have gone over, pull them up. Put the petals in the dustbin to prevent an outbreak of tulip fire disease.

PESTS/DISEASE	SYMPTOMS	TREATMENTS
Cuckoo spit	Frothy, white masses around stems protecting colonies of froghoppers. These sap-feeders distort young growth.	Squash insects by hand and hose off gently with water.
Grey mould (Botrytis)	Spots then fluffy mould and rot on flowers, leaves or stems. Common in wet conditions.	Increase ventilation, destroy affected areas, replacing badly diseased plants. Improve air circulation by removing lower leaves or spacing further apart. Spray with fungicide.
Powdery mildew	White, powdery fungus on leaves encouraged by dry conditions at roots.	Water regularly; pick off diseased sections; spray with fungicide.
Wilt	Plant wilting when potting compost is evenly watered; common to asters, zinnias, poppies and snapdragons.	Repot affected plant with fresh compost, or discard and replace with different species.
Rust	Raised brown, orange or yellow spots on leaves or stems; common on snapdragons and pelargoniums.	Remove and discard affected parts. Spray with fungicide.
Leaf spots	Diseased marks on leaves. Spots common to pansies; concentric rings to carnations; and blotches to columbines.	Pick off and destroy diseased sections. Spray with appropriate fungicide.
Virus	Varied symptoms affecting flowers, leaves or stems: from stunting and distortion to colour changes and mottling (mosaic virus). Few viruses are beneficial.	Untreatable so remove plant and destroy; do not use for cuttings. Control aphids to reduce transfer of infection.
Tulip fire disease	Brown, scorched leaf tips leading to rot; spots on leaves and flowers; black capsules on bulbs.	Gather and throw away or burn infected bulbs, petals and leaves.

The Ultimate Container Plant Directory

Star quality plants
Dwarf conifers
Dwarf daffodils (*Narcissus*)
Dwarf tulips (*Tulipa*)
Fatsia
Fuchsias
Geraniums (*Pelargonium*)
Hostas
Japanese maples (*Acer japonicum, A. palmatum*)
Lilies (*Lilium*)
Pansies
  (*Viola x wittrockiana*)
Tomatoes
'Yak' rhododendrons
  (*R. yakushimanum* and
  hybrids)

Scented flowers
Chocolate cosmos
  (*Cosmos atrosanguineus*)
Daphne odora
  'Aureomarginata'
Deciduous azaleas
  (*Rhododendron*)
Heliotrope (*Heliotropium*)
Hyacinths (*Hyacinthus*)
Lily 'Star Gazer'
Petunias
Pinks (*Dianthus*)
Tobacco plants (*Nicotiana*)
Wallflowers (*Erysimum*)

Scented leaves
Chamomile
  (*Chamaemelum nobile*)
Curry plant (*Helichrysum italicum*)
Eau de Cologne mint
  (*Mentha x piperita*
  'Citrata')

Lavenders (*Lavandula*)
Lemon balm (*Melissa officinalis*)
Lemon verbena (*Aloysia triphylla*)
Pineapple sage (*Salvia rutilans*)
Rosemary (*Rosmarinus*)
Scented-leaved geraniums
  (*Pelargonium*)
Thyme (*Thymus*)

Rapid growers for quick effect
Anthemis punctata subsp.
  cupaniana
Balcon ivy-leaved
  geraniums (*Pelargonium*)
Bidens
Cosmos
Helichrysum petiolare
Many hardy annuals
Mint (*Mentha*)
Sunflowers (*Helianthus*)
Surfinia petunias (*P.*
  'Surfinia')
Trailing nasturtiums

Plants to perform a floral marathon
Begonia 'Non Stop'
Brachycomes
Busy lizzies (*Impatiens*)
Diascias
Felicias
Fuchsias
Lobelia
Marigolds (*Tagetes*)
Pansies
  (*Viola x wittrockiana*)
Scaevolas

Year-round interest
Acer palmatum
  'Osakazuki'
Box (*Buxus*)
Choisyas
Fuchsia 'Thalia'
Hostas
Lenten rose (*Helleborus orientalis*)
Spurge (*Euphorbia charantias* subsp. *wulfenii*)
Winter heathers (*Erica*)

Acid-loving plants
Azaleas
Callunas
Camellias
Gaultherias
Leucothöe
Pieris
Rhododendrons
Winter heathers (*Erica*)*
Witch hazel (*Hamamelis*)
* some species only

Shade-tolerant plants
Busy lizzies (*Impatiens*)
Cyclamen
Ferns
Fuchsias
Hostas
Ivies (*Hedera*)
Monkey musk (*Mimulus*)
Rhododendrons
Spotted laurel (*Aucuba japonica* 'Crotonifolia')
Tobacco plants (*Nicotiana*)

Drought-tolerant plants
Cacti and succulents
Festuca grasses

Houseleeks (*Sempervivum*)
Ivies (*Hedera*)
Lavenders (*Lavandula*)
Lewisias
Pines (*Pinus*)
Pinks (*Dianthus*)
Scented-leaved geraniums
  (*Pelargonium*)
Stonecrop (*Sedum*)
Thyme (*Thymus*)
Yuccas

Permanent container plants grown for their flowers
Angels' trumpets
  (*Brugmansia*, syn. *Datura*)
Camellias
Clematis
Fuchsias
Hebes
Hydrangeas
Pieris
Rhododendrons
Skimmia japonica 'Rubella'

Permanent container plants grown for foliage
Bamboos
Box (*Buxus*) topiary
Cordylines
Dwarf conifers
Euonymus
Fatsias
Ferns including tree ferns
Hostas
Japanese maple (*Acer japonicum, A. palmatum*)
Phormiums
Spotted laurel (*Aucuba japonica*)

Small trees
Aralias
Gleditsia triacanthos 'Rubylace'
Japanese maple (*Acer japonicum, A. palmatum*)
Sorbus x hostii
Sumachs (*Rhus*)
Weeping birch (*Betula pendula* 'Youngii')
Weeping cotoneasters
Weeping pussy willow (*Salix caprea* 'Kilmarnock')

Climbers*
Clematis
Cup-and-saucer vine (*Cobaea scandens*)
Honeysuckles (*Lonicera*)
Ivies (*Hedera*)
Morning glory (*Ipomoea purpurea*)
Summer jasmine (*Jasminum officinale*)
Sweet peas (*Lathyrus odoratus*)
Winter jasmine (*Jasminum nudiflorum*)

* some may eventually outgrow their pot

Trailing plants
Bidens
Brachycomes
Convolvulus sabatius
Diascias
Fuchsia 'Autumnale'
Helichrysum petiolare 'Limelight'
Lobelia
Petunia Surfinia 'Blue Vein'
Scaevolas
Verbena 'Pink Parfait'
V. 'Sissinghurst'

Exotic ornamental shrubs for a sunny patio*
Adam's needle (*Yucca filamentosa* 'Bright Edge')
Angels' trumpets (*Brugmansia*, syn. *Datura*)
Bottlebrush (*Callistemon*)
Cabbage palm (*Cordyline australis* 'Atropurpurea')
Camellia sasanqua
Coronilla valentina subsp. *glauca*
Dwarf pomegranate (*Punica granatum* var. *nana*)
False castor oil plant (*Fatsia japonica* 'Variegata')
Flowering maples (*Abutilon* 'Ashford Red', *A.* 'Kentish Belle')
Glory bush (*Tibouchina urvilleana*)
Karo (*Pittosporum crassifolium* 'Variegatum')
Lemon (*Citrus x meyeri* 'Meyer')
Lemon verbena (*Aloysia triphylla*)
Mimosa (*Acacia dealbata*)
Mimulus aurantiacus
New Zealand flax (*Phormium* 'Sundowner' and other striped varieties)
New Zealand tea tree (*Leptospermum scoparium* 'Red Damask')
Ozothamnus rosmarinifolius 'Silver Jubilee'
Parrot's bill (*Clianthus puniceus*)
Sweet bay (*Laurus nobilis*)

* overwinter in a frost-free greenhouse

Tender or half-hardy plants
Angels' trumpets (*Brugmansia*, syn. *Datura*)
Argyranthemums
Brachycomes
Cannas
Convolvulus sabatius
Dahlias
Diascias*
Felicias
Fuchsias
Geraniums (*Pelargonium*)
Helichrysum petiolare
Lobelia
Lotus
Osteospermums
Scaevolas
Trailing verbena

* some varieties are virtually hardy

Dwarf bulbs
Crocus
Cyclamen
Daffodils (*Narcissus*)*
Fritillaria
Glory of the snow (*Chionodoxa*)
Grape hyacinth (*Muscari*)
Iris reticulata
Scillas
Snowdrops (*Galanthus*)
Tulips (*Tulipa*)*

* some varieties only

Herbs
Basil (*Ocimum basilicum*)
Chives (*Allium schoenoprasum*)
Coriander (*Coriandrum*)
Curry plant (*Helichrysum italicum*)
Lemon balm (*Melissa officinalis*)
Marjoram (*Origanum*)

Mint (*Mentha*)
Parsley (*Petroselinum*)
Rosemary (*Rosmarinus*)
Sage (*Salvia officinalis*)
Sweet bay (*Laurus nobilis*)
Thyme (*Thymus*)

Ornamental salad vegetables to grow with herbs
Dwarf bush tomatoes
Ornamental cabbage
Ornamental kale
Peppers
Purple-podded, dwarf beans
Red-leaved lettuce
Ruby chard
Trailing tomatoes
Variegated nasturtiums
Yellow-podded, dwarf beans

House plants that can be stood outside in summer
Aspidistras
Begonias
Busy lizzies (*Impatiens*)
Cacti and other succulents
Christmas cactus (*Schlumbergera x buckleyi*)
Coleus
Jasmine (*Jasminum polyanthum*)
Spider plant (*Chlorophytum comosum*)
Tradescantia
Umbrella plant (*Cyperus alternifolius*)
Winter cherry (*Solanum capsicastrum*)

INDEX

AUTHOR'S ACKNOWLEDGEMENTS

Sourcing pots, tubs and containers
Good places to buy pots, tubs and containers are garden centres, DIY outlets and
garden shows or direct from the manufacturers. If you trace those made in the United
Kingdom back to their source of origin you will get a valuable insight into
how they are produced.

**Containers used in the following recipes were provided by the
manufacturer or supplier named:**

Hyacinth parade (pp.36–37) . . . . Bradstone Pots & Planters
Mellow yellow (pp.44–45) . . . . . Errington-Reay Ltd
Wedgwood (pp.46–47) . . . . Bradstone Pots & Planters
Summer magic (pp.48–49) . . . . . Whichford Pottery
Summer pastels (pp.50–51) . . . . Hampshire Garden Craft
Gracious herbaceous (pp.52–53) . Pembridge Terracotta
Dapper dahlias (pp.58–59) . . . . . C.H. Brannam Ltd

Cottage pot (pp.62–63) . . . . C.H. Brannam Ltd
A class act (pp.64–65) . . . . C.H. Brannam Ltd
Blazeaway begonias (pp.66–67) . . Bradstone Pots & Planters
Trail blazers (pp.74–75) . . . . Hampshire Garden Craft
Ice & lemon (pp.76–77) . . . . C.H. Brannam Ltd
Monkey business (pp.78–79) . . . Errington-Reay Ltd
Roses revealed (pp.92–93) . . . . . . Haddonstone Ltd

All other containers featured in this book are widely available from garden-product
stockists, car boot sales, junk shops and auctions.

All photographs were taken by myself.

I would like to thank: Shirley Patton, Maggie Aldred and Joanna Chisholm for their
ideas, enthusiasm and attention to detail; and Nicky Jones for helping with the care
and maintenance section, and for growing and posing for photographs. Most of the
recipes were grown using Arthur Bowers Multipurpose potting compost.

ADDRESSES
Contact for details of stockists/availability

Bradstone Pots & Planters,
Camas Building Materials,
Hulland Ward,
Ashbourne,
Derbyshire DE6 3ET
tel. 01335 372222

C.H. Brannam Ltd,
Roundswell Industrial Estate,
Barnstaple,
Devon EX31 3NJ
tel. 01271 43035

Errington-Reay Ltd,
Tyneside Pottery Works,
Bardon Mill,
Hexham,
Northumberland NE47 7HU
tel. 01434 344245

Haddonstone Ltd,
The Forge House,
East Haddon,
Northants NN6 8DB
tel. 01604 770711

Hampshire Garden Craft,
Rake Industries,
Rake,
Petersfield,
Hants GU31 5DR
tel. 01730 785182

Pembridge Terracotta,
Pembridge,
Leominster,
Herefordshire HR6 9HB
tel. 01544 388696

Whichford Pottery,
Whichford,
Shipston-on-Stour,
Warwickshire CV36 5PG
tel. 01608 684416